NEW DRUGS

An Insider's Guide to
the FDA's New Drug Approval Process

for Scientists, Investors and Patients

Cover design by Bruce Kenselaar.

ISBN: 1-4196-9961-X

ISBN-13: 9781419699610

Library of Congress Control Number: 2009901880

Pharmaceutical Special Projects Group, LLC (PSPG) Publishing, New York, NY

Visit www.newdrugsbook.com to order additional copies.

NEW DRUGS

An Insider's Guide to
the FDA's New Drug Approval Process

for Scientists, Investors and Patients

Lawrence T. Friedhoff MD, PhD, FACP

Table of Contents

Chapter 7 - Phase III Human Studies   65

Chapter 8 - Late Stage Activities   87

Chapter 9 - A Word on Phase IV Studies   97

Chapter 10 - NDA Submission and The NDA
Submission Team   99

Preface

I AM WRITING this book after almost a quarter of a century of deep involvement in the process called drug development; this consists of obtaining scientific data that will allow a new drug to be approved for marketing by governmental agencies like FDA. During this almost 25-year period, the number of new drugs approved annually by FDA has dwindled to a fraction of its former value. However, during this same period I was getting more and more drugs approved. I have written this book in the hopes that it will help others get new drugs approved quickly and efficiently as well and that this will contribute in some small way to reversing the decline in new drug approvals.

This book is also provided as a guide for more passive participants in the drug development process, including people who play an often less direct, but essential, role in the progress that drug development delivers to our society, such as investors and pharmaceutical stock analysts. Finally, I hope that this book will help patients have a better understanding of the way new drugs are approved and the strengths and weaknesses of the information collected during the research and approval process.

The knowledge I share has come after much struggle and, sometimes, bitter experience. Since there is no formal school that teaches drug development in a practical way, I have had to fend for myself much of the time; picking up knowledge from such experts as I could find along the way.

Early in my career, I had the good fortune to work at Squibb Corporation at a time when some of the world's best drug developers were also there, making revolutionary advances in drug discovery and development. It is a sad and interesting part of Squibb's history that the principle actors in the development of some of the last century's most important "blockbuster" drugs, drugs that have revolutionized the modern world, remain unknown and little appreciated, their creations having been relegated to profit and loss statements and net-present-value calculations. This failure to accurately recognize the people and processes that create the value in the pharmaceutical business is a very real and consistent force that must be recognized and properly managed as part of the drug development process.

Thus, this guide will not confine itself to purely scientific or regulatory issues, but will include the other business and practical concerns that must, in my opinion, be kept in mind by a successful drug developer. Such concerns are also of importance to investors and financial analysts since the narrow personal motivations of the individuals involved in drug development frequently trump scientific and regulatory considerations in determining the outcome and ultimate financial return of the development process.

This book primarily discusses the development of completely new drugs, called New Chemical Entities ("NCEs" or synonymously New Molecular Entities, "NMEs"). These are drugs that have never before been approved for marketing. However, this is not the only kind of drug product that can be developed. Chapter 13 and Appendix 1 give brief discussions of the other types and how they compare to the development of NCEs. Following the academic discussion of the drug development process, I have also included case studies and personal anecdotes that help elucidate the general principles I have outlined in the first part of this manuscript. I have also included a brief glossary of technical terms, a key regulatory guidance document (Appendix 3), and a brief discussion of manufacturing issues (Appendix 4), an often neglected but critical element of drug development.

Appendix 2 discusses some common misconceptions the general public has about the pharmaceutical business but which the industry spokespeople have not been able to clarify. I happen to think these misconceptions ultimately slow scientific progress hurting both companies and patients in need of new therapies.

Whatever your motivation for reading it, I hope you will find this guide as interesting, informative, and profitable as I have found my career in drug development.

Finally, I would like to give an important cautionary note: Drug development, particularly, the development of a completely new drug, is an extremely complex and expensive undertaking. Each year thousands of companies try and almost all of them fail. In fact, although my colleagues and I at Pharmaceutical Special Projects Group have always been successful, most drug development professionals go through an entire career without ever seeing one of their products approved for marketing. Because the process is so challenging and the risks so high, drug development should ALWAYS be handled by the most competent and experienced personnel. So, don't try this at home without guidance from an experienced professional with a proven track record of hands-on success at drug development. And when hiring personnel to handle drug development, don't be seduced into choosing the least expensive. Choose as though you are selecting a surgeon to do your cardiac bypass surgery; because in drug development, as in cardiac surgery, there isn't much room for error.

Chapter 1 - What is a Drug?

HUMANS ARE LATECOMERS in using chemicals to prevent and treat disease. Long before apes stood erect, plants were synthesizing molecules to perform the same basic functions that we use drugs for. In fact, many of the drugs we use today are derived from molecules used as "drugs" by plants. Plants use these molecules primarily to protect themselves from parasites and for other similar purposes. Plant-derived drugs include, caffeine, nicotine, digitalis glycosides, penicillin antibiotics (derived from molds), opiates, the HMG-CoA Reductase inhibitor cholesterol-lowering agents (derived from fungi), a number of anti-cancer agents and many others.

Obviously, these molecules made by plants existed for millennia before they were recognized as having potential utility as drugs. One can legitimately ask if these substances were "drugs" before their utility was recognized. In the view of most current drug development practitioners (and drug regulators) the answer is "No." Just because a molecule with drug-like activity (for example, the ability to kill bacteria) exists, it cannot be considered a "drug" until its activity is recognized by humans. Furthermore, recognition of a substance's utility involves not just recognition that it possesses activity but also identification of the way in which is should be used (for example, duration of treatment, route of administration, etc.).

History is replete with examples of molecules that were excellent drugs but that were initially used in the wrong way or for the wrong condition, thereby greatly limiting or obviating their use by the medical profession. A good example is minoxidil. During my medical training, orally administered minoxidil was used as a treatment for high blood pressure. Although it was quite effective, it was reserved for patients with extremely resistant high blood pressure as a last ditch treatment after every other drug had failed, because of its unusual side-effect, hirsuitism (unwanted hair growth). Years later, someone had the interesting idea of using minoxidil to treat hair loss by administering it topically, thus maximizing its activity on the hair follicle and minimizing its effect on blood pressure. Minoxidil thus became a treatment for hair-loss with the potential for side effects on blood pressure rather than a treatment for high blood pressure with a side-effect of hair growth. In contrast with its very limited use as a treatment for high blood pressure, minoxidil is widely used for treatment of hair loss. Thus, once the appropriate use and topical method of administration were identified, the characterization of minoxidil was completely altered, and it became a very successful and essentially "new" drug. It can be found on the shelves of essentially every pharmacy in the developed world.

The minoxidil example, and many others that could be cited, point out the importance of recognizing that a "drug" is comprised of four parts: the drug substance (active ingredient) the physical form (e.g., tablet, topical solution, solution for injection, etc.), the route and frequency of administration and condition it is used to treat. In the language used by government regulators, a "drug" is the active ingredient (drug substance, active pharmaceutical ingredient, API) together with its physical embodiment as a drug product (tablet, capsule, etc.) together with its method of administration (oral, intramuscular injection, once daily, twice daily, etc.) and the condition for which it is used (in regulatory parlance, the product's "indication").

Technically, from the regulatory point of view, a "drug" is the actual drug product approved by the regulatory body [generally, the approved product includes a specified range of inactive ingredients (excipients) and allowed impurities and degradants, along with its approved Package Insert (in the US) or Summary of Product Characteristics (in Europe)], together with the approved labels and packaging for the drug product. The Package Insert plus the actual labels on the drug product package are referred to as the "approved labeling." The Package Insert contains the key information about the drug described above; namely the structure of the drug substance, its physical embodiment (tablet, capsule, etc. in the "How Supplied" section), its recommended route of administration and dose regimen ("Dosage and Administration" section) and its approved uses ("Indications and Usage" section). It also summarizes the most important results of the development process that will be described in the following sections.

The Approved Labeling is important because the information contained in the Package Insert is generally the only information that can be used by the manufacturer in advertising to promote the product. Although a drug product can be used for purposes other than those included in the approved Package Insert, this use is considered "off label" and cannot, in general, be encouraged by the manufacturer. For example a manufacturer cannot allow its agents, such as sales representatives to promote these off-label uses to doctors, hospitals or pharmacies. Failure to adhere to these rules can result in significant civil and or criminal liability. (See the example of criminal misbranding in Chapter 18). In addition, key adverse-event information in the approved Package Insert must be included in any promotional material. This makes support of the approved Package Insert a function of the drug approval process, driving the kind of studies conducted during development and frequently being a bone of contention between the pharmaceutical company and regulators.

Thus, obtaining regulatory approval for the desired Package Insert can confer an important commercial advantage to the pharmaceutical sponsor. Conversely, failure to achieve the desired product labeling can hobble both promotion and use of the product once it is approved. Because of the central role of product labeling in determining the medical and economic value of a product, obtaining the desired product labeling is an important objective of the development process described in the remainder of this document.

Chapter 2 - Background

Economic Considerations

NO DISCUSSION OF the drug development process would be complete or understandable without putting it in its proper business and cultural context. With the possible exception of the energy business, the pharmaceutical industry is probably the most profitable industry in the world. Judging by earnings per employee, most pharmaceutical companies are extremely profitable compared with other business enterprises.

Successful development of a major new pharmaceutical product typically returns revenue that is approximately 500 times the development investment. In general, pre-tax profit is 50% or more of revenue; thus, successful drug development is capable of generating an after-tax return on investment of about 15,000% (assuming a 40% tax rate). This extremely high potential return is what drives investments in the pharmaceutical business.

The high financial stakes also drive the abuses of trust that often accompany any activity involving a large amount of money. In my experience, the struggle to control and/or take this potential return for personal benefit is the most common cause of failure of the drug development process, rivaled only by the misrepresentation of scientific data for the purpose of exaggerating the chances of successful development. Both forces can have profound effects on the development process. The results often mimic the outcome of the famous movie "The Treasure of the Sierra Madre" where, once the treasure is in hand, it is lost due to the squabbling and dishonesty of the treasure seekers. This is a recurring theme in the pharmaceutical business and must always be kept in mind by both active participants in the development process and passive investors. It is my hope that this book will help improve the efficiency of the development process by alerting participants to these and other potential pitfalls.

As in any business where the potential returns are very high, the risks are substantial. Thus, a core competency of a successful pharmaceutical company is management of development risk. While there are many methods of risk management that have been shown to be successful over time, in my experience adherence to the methods I will outline in this book, is critical to a thriving pharmaceutical business. It might be expected that such rules would be codified and rigorously followed given the high stakes involved in pharmaceutical development. In my experience this is often not true. Management of the development process is often driven by the desire of various constituencies to minimize the apparent risks of development so as to justify further investment, including their paychecks, bonuses and pensions.

Thus, a key goal of management should always be to minimize the opportunity (and therefore temptation) for such concerns to drive the company's development budget. This is often not a simple task, particularly, if the management attempting it does not have a deep understanding of the development process. Thus, a key concern for everyone involved in the development process is the skill with which upper management assesses the potential risks and rewards of the many development opportunities available to a typical company.

This is an important concern for investors as well. Concern should always be raised when the management of a company has little concrete development experience. This is common in the pharmaceutical industry where many CEOs and board chairpersons are lawyers, accountants, or MBAs with limited scientific training and often no drug development experience. The same concern exists when the top management's scientific credentials are unrelated to drug development. Thus, companies that are dominated by academic leaders can come to a poor end if their academic experience is not supplemented by experienced drug development personnel (although there are also notable exceptions). This is because, like most endeavors in life, success in drug development requires education and experience in drug development. Outstanding achievements in other fields of endeavor are, in my experience usually not correlated to success in the drug development process.

When management does not have significant experience in drug development, it is key to have some way of evaluating the plans and progress of the drug development process that is not biased by the financial and other personal pressures that affect internal company employees. Fulfilling this function is one reason I started the Pharmaceutical Special Projects Group, LLC. As a team for over 15 years, the group has always been successful in getting its drugs approved and can therefore maximize the chance that a client's product will also be successful.

Managers with outstanding records of successful drug development often repeat their performance again and again. Their success is usually based on the rigorous implementation of simple rules that, with proper support from management, generally lead to repeated successful drug marketing approvals and large profits for all involved. I will outline these rules in the following sections, with the caveat that while the rules are generally simple, implementing them in aggregate is generally very complicated. Successful implementation requires a detailed understanding of the data available for the particular drug being developed along with the skills to implement the procedures required for successful development in a high-pressure environment.

While I am hopeful that an individual with some experience in drug development can improve his or her skills using the methods outlined in this book, it is not intended to be an instruction manual for the completely naive. Drug development is far too complex and involves too many intangible skills to be learned from a book and the stakes are usually too high to be entrusted to unproven personnel. However, this book will provide a general framework on which a novice can organize his or her own experiences and technical knowledge.

It is absolutely critical that a CEO, COO or president without hands-on development experience who finds him/herself in charge of a company engaged in drug development find the appropriate experienced staff to manage the development process. These people will be exceptionally difficult to supervise by managers lacking the technical expertise needed to objectively evaluate plans and progress. In this case, an experienced outside consulting group, like

Pharmaceutical Special Projects Group, LLC, with a long, successful track record may play a key management support role. When selecting outside support, be very careful. The range of abilities available in the marketplace is very wide, and as mentioned above, people with many years of experience may have never been responsible for a successful product. Although I have met many capable, intelligent drug development people over the years, I have also encountered remarkable discrepancies between "paper" qualifications and actual abilities. This disparity is particularly pronounced when a candidate comes from a very large company where employees have very circumscribed responsibilities and knowledge.

It is my hope that readers who are not part of the pharmaceutical industry will also derive benefit from this book: pharmaceutical investors at all levels from large institutional to small private may gain some insight into the qualities important to choosing a company to invest in, and the casual reader will gain a better understanding of what it takes to bring a drug to market, and the important role that government regulation plays in making sure that a company's economic interest does not conflict with its ethics.

Risk Management

At its heart, the drug development process is an exercise in risk management. Successful drug developers are skilled at estimating and mitigating risk. They know how to prioritize the development process so the maximum amount of risk is eliminated at the smallest possible cost in time and money. Doing this successfully is very dependent on the skills and personalities of the people involved in the development process. Thus, it is important to know what kind of personality to look for in drug development personnel.

A successful drug developer often has a nervous energy that is apparent from across the room. He or she has no tolerance for nebulous statements and is typically fanatically concerned with honesty, often to the point of committing social faux pas. Obsessive-compulsive disorder, within limits, is a powerful asset, since successful development requires meticulous attention to details and the ability to focus intensely on the task at hand. The polished, well-dressed, socially-adept individual is less likely to be successful as a drug developer although they may be very valuable in other contexts. A very expensive watch may be a sign of high risk. Look for one on the wrist of the head of business development not the head of drug development.

Key Personnel

In this section I will outline a typical way of organizing key personnel. As may be gleaned from the prior section, finding the correct people both in terms of skills and psychological makeup is critical to successful drug development.

Clear delegation of responsibilities and the parallel assignment of authorities is also essential. Since drug development is very complex, it can be accomplished only by breaking it down into manageable parts delegated to responsible individuals, as the following Table summarizes.

Implementation of the functions listed in the table will be discussed in more detail in the following sections. However, the personnel are introduced here to give a human framework to what will follow. This framework is critically important because having the correct people is essential to successful drug development.

Title	Typical Educational Background	Typical Experience	Typical Responsibilities	Typical Authorities
Project Leader	MD and/or PhD	Successful management of a prior development program resulting in marketing approval	Selection of other members of the Project Team. Division of responsibilities and authorities. Dispute resolution and priority assignment	Control of the project's budget and authority over all supporting services needed for successful development
Regulatory Affairs	BA, MA and/or PhD	At least 5 years of regulatory experience covering all aspects of the development process (e.g. manufacturing, non-clinical, clinical pharmacology and clinical trials). Successful interaction with major regulatory authorities.	Review of all activities with respect to compliance with laws and guidelines. Establishment of quality control procedures	Veto power over all activities deemed to violate laws or regulations or to compromise the quality of the development project
Manufacturing	PhD	At least 5 years experience managing a program for a successful new drug. This should include both GMP and non-GMP manufacturing and scale-up to commercial size batches.	Management of all manufacturing. Coordination of manufacturing activities with Non-clinical, Clinical Pharmacology and Clinical Development to assure that drug supplies are available as needed. Management of the drug product and substance stability program.	Budget, personnel assignment, and priority setting for all manufacturing activities
Non-clinical	PhD	At least 5 years experience managing non-clinical including responsibility for a successful new drug.	Management of all non-clinical activities including efficacy pharmacology, safety pharmacology, toxicology and metabolism studies. Interaction with the Clinical Pharmacology person to assure integration of the animal and human pharmacology programs.	Budget, personnel assignment, and final decision making for all non-clinical activities

Title	Typical Educational Background	Typical Experience	Typical Responsibilities	Typical Authorities
Clinical Pharmacology	MA and/or PhD	At least 5 years of successful clinical pharmacology experience including a successful new drug approval. Experience dealing with regulatory authorities.	Responsibility for all clinical pharmacology studies. Interaction with the non-clinical person to assure integration of the human and animal pharmacology programs	Budget, personnel assignment, and final decision-making for all clinical pharmacology activities
Clinical Development	MD	At least 5 years of successful Phase III experience including involvement with a successful new drug approval. Experience dealing with regulatory authorities.	Management of all Phase III trials. Coordination of Phase III program with the Clinical Pharmacology and Non-clinical studies needed for support.	Design and implementation of all Phase III clinical trials including design of study protocols. Budget and hiring responsibility for all Phase III related personnel, excluding contract research organizations.
Project Management and Finance	MA and/or CPA	At least 5 years of experience in project management and finance, including financial reporting	Review of all expenditures and projections of all timelines and budgets. Review of all contracts to assure favorable terms.	Final approval of all plans and expenditures.
Clinical Operations	BA and/or MA	At least 7 years of clinical operations experience including management of the successful development of a new drug	Selection of clinical study sites and contract research organizations	Final decision making authority for study sites and contract research organizations. Budget approval for all clinical study related expenses

As can be seen, only about 8 people are needed for a successful project team. The key is to get the correct people. Increasing the number of people does not compensate for having inexperienced or inappropriate personnel. In fact, having excess personnel magnifies the deficiencies of each by tending to blur lines of responsibility and authority.

Although many other people are an essential part of the development process, (including plant workers who make the drug, field monitors who manage the clinical sites, regulatory staff who prepare and mail regulatory documents and clinical site personnel who find recruit and treat volunteers and patients) it is the members of the project team who will have the greatest effect on the outcome of a development program and who have the greatest exposure to management and the public.

Chapter 3 - Finding Potential Drugs: The Initial Preclinical Evaluation

Practical Evaluation of New Product Candidates

THE MAIN SUBJECT of this book is a description of practical methods for obtaining marketing approval for an active ingredient that has already been identified as the likely basis for a commercial product (an activity commonly called "drug development") rather than the process of discovering such products. This is not to say that drug discovery is unimportant. On the contrary, it is the basis of success in the pharmaceutical industry. However, most of my career has been oriented around selecting products I thought likely to be successful and implementing a development program that resulted in the approval of a successful commercial product. Therefore most of this book is dedicated to that process. One of the most important parts of the process is selecting a product to develop. This chapter is devoted to the initial product selection process.

As mentioned in Chapter 1, the ultimate marketing of a drug will be limited by the information included in the Package Insert (or non-US equivalent). Thus, the activities summarized in the rest of this book should be evaluated in terms of their potential contribution to the approved Package Insert and the market that the Package Insert will support. If the likely approved Package Insert will meet an important unmet medical need, the product should be pursued vigorously. If the Package Insert will not meet an important unmet medical need or worse, if the data suggest no reasonable Package Insert is possible, the product should be dropped from development and replaced.

One common misconception is that development projects are difficult to find. During the course of over two decades in the pharmaceutical business, I have evaluated many hundreds and perhaps more than a thousand projects; typically one or more a week. A number of these could be or have been successfully developed into new drugs. During the course of a day, I often have one or more ideas for projects that could potentially merit development. The challenge for a drug developer like myself (as opposed to a drug discoverer) is to select the product that is most likely to be commercially successful. This is especially important because the drug-development process is very expensive, and resources naturally need to be employed in the most efficient manner.

This chapter summarizes simple criteria for product selection that, in my experience, lead to great commercial success. Although the criteria are relatively simple, the reader is urged not to underestimate the difficulty of implementing them, especially in a large complex organization. As a result of this difficulty, the process of valuing potential products is often extremely inefficient. This can lead to major misallocations of resources toward products that ultimately fail in development and away from products that could be and sometimes do become successful commercial products. The failure to accurately value development program(s) probably has many causes. However, in my experience, the main cause is the failure to enforce a selection method that values projects in terms of their ability to fulfill unmet medical needs. An unmet medical need represents a group of patients whose treatment could be improved in a meaningful way by a new drug product. Products that can improve the care of such patients generally lead to large profits. However, in the absence of clear direction, many other objectives can cloud the decision-making process. For example, a company's stock may appreciate on the basis of hopes for a new product being considered for development. This may lead to pressure to avoid evaluations of the product that could produce negative data that may lower the perceived value of the product and hence the company's stock. Thus, evaluations that are needed for regulatory approval may be delayed beyond the time they should be done in an efficient development plan. Similarly, products may be advanced to stages that are unwarranted simply because this advancement increases the apparent value of the product in the minds of the investing public and therefore can enhance the company's stock price.

Another problem is competition among employees involved in the drug discovery process. Naturally, each wants their product to be advanced in development as this gives their product a chance to help patients and increases their visibility and chances for promotion. This is a particular problem when it comes to comparing products available for in-licensing with those discovered internally. In most companies, potential in-licensing products are evaluated by the same group that is engaged in discovering and evaluating new internally discovered products. In many cases, such personnel are reluctant to recommend in-licensing of a product that will divert attention and resources away from products they may already be involved with and which, all things being equal, they are likely to value above development candidates discovered by others.

It is the task of good management to mitigate the effects of these distortions of the decision-making process. Based on the many multi-billion dollar mistakes I have seen, it appears that controlling these confounding factors is very difficult. However, companies that can do so are generally extremely successful.

General Considerations

Choosing the Indication

The discussion that follows assumes that a potential drug candidate has a well-defined, single indication. Although this is true in many cases, most new molecular entities have multiple potential indications. In this case each indication should be evaluated separately, using the criteria laid out in this section. Once adequate analyses are in hand, each indication can be prioritized based on its estimated chances for successful development and its ability to satisfy an unmet medical need.

It is important to remember that if the evaluations for an indication fail, financial and political support for the project will likely decrease dramatically making it impossible to evaluate alternate indications. So it is important to choose the initial indication or indications carefully.

Mechanism of Action

Typically, new drugs are first characterized by identifying their proposed mechanism of action. A proposed new drug may bind to a receptor in the body that is well known to be involved in a disease process. An important determinant of the chance for success of the putative new drug is the robustness of the relationship between the proposed mechanism of action and influence on the disease process. If there are other drugs with the same mechanism of action that are well proven to be effective, it is more likely that a new drug will also be effective. Products with an exciting "new" mechanism of action, are inherently more developmentally risky than those with proven mechanisms. Thus, the potential reward for successful development of a product with a novel mechanism of action should be much greater than the reward for a product whose mechanism of action has already been shown to be conclusively associated with clinical effectiveness. An example of a well proven mechanism of action are the drugs that inhibit an enzyme known as HMG CoA Reductase, e..g. Mevacor®, Lipitor® and Zocor®. These enzyme inhibitors reduce LDL cholesterol in animals and people with a high degree of reliability. Thus, such an enzyme inhibitor is very likely to be effective in people if it shows efficacy in in vitro and in vivo animal models.

Potency

The effects of drugs are generally dependent on the amount used and therefore careful attention should be paid to the amount of drug required in order to obtain a desired effect. In general, drug concentrations in the pico or nanomolar range are desirable, because most molecules do not have meaningful toxicity at such concentrations. Thus, with luck, such a product will have clinical adverse effects related only to its mechanism of action at the dilute concentrations required for efficacy. For example, a drug designed to lower blood sugar in diabetics might have the side-effect of lowering blood sugar too much, but hopefully would not have other unrelated side effects like liver toxicity or cardiac arrhythmias. If the concentrations required to demonstrate efficacy go above the micromolar range, it is less likely that the product will prove useful as a drug to be absorbed into the body because the amount required for dosing may prove impractically large. Furthermore, at such concentrations many substances have unrelated effects that may be undesirable.

Possible exceptions to this potency standard include drugs that will be applied topically. Very high concentrations at the site of application can sometimes be achieved with topical administration. However, the potential for unwanted toxicity is still present even with topical administration. Thus, in general, the EC_{50} (a measure of the potency of a drug in solution) should be in the micromolar range or lower, with a nanomolar or lower being best.

Metabolites

Metabolites are molecules created by the body as it breaks down a drug. It is often possible for a skilled medicinal chemist or biochemist to assess the potential for metabolism of a new molecule based on its chemical structure prior to actual laboratory metabolism measurements. It is important to consider metabolism because the body is exposed not just to the product administered but also to all the new molecules that result as the body breaks it down via the process of metabolism. Each metabolite, therefore, is essentially a new drug with the potential for both side effects and efficacy. If the metabolite is more efficacious than the drug being tested, the metabolite should, in general, be used instead. If it is significantly less potent, then it provides only the potential for side effects and is undesirable. Furthermore, metabolism increases the potential for interactions with other drugs patients may be taking, an important source of drug toxicity in clinical practice. Thus, products with few or no metabolites are generally more desirable than those with many metabolites.

Initial Evaluations of Efficacy and Safety

Aside from the general considerations summarized in the sections above, a rigorous evaluation of the value of a drug candidate must be based on separate evaluations of its likely efficacy and safety. These are supplemented with an assessment of drug levels in blood and assessments of the metabolic transformation. Once reliable data are in hand, a risk benefit analysis, comparing assessments of efficacy and safety, can be done and the likely value of the product can be estimated. The following section describes the evaluations of potential efficacy that are typically done prior to human studies. This is followed by a description of typical safety evaluations, assessments of blood drug levels and metabolism and finally, by a method for doing a risk/benefit analysis prior to the initiation of human studies.

Evaluations of Efficacy
Evaluation of Efficacy *In Vitro*

As a general rule, potential new drug products are evaluated in laboratory systems before human studies are conducted. Typically, the initial laboratory studies involve evaluation *in vitro* (that is "in glass", i.e. in living cells or tissue in a glass container, but not in a whole living animal). *In vitro* evaluation eliminates some of the complexities involved in studies of whole animals and generally gives more reproducible data, thereby reducing the number of experiments required to reach reliable conclusions. For example, a compound may be active *in vitro* even though it may not be absorbed following oral administration to a whole animal. This information is valuable because at the earliest stages of the drug discovery process, absorption may not be as important as identifying an effective way of modifying the desired cellular target.

Once a molecule with pharmacologic activity at the desired cellular target is identified, absorption can be addressed by a variety of means, including altered routes of administration (injection for example) or modifications of the molecule that increase absorption. There are many other issues that cloud the extrapolation of *in vitro* effects to the human clinical situation. For example, the whole body may metabolize (alter the drug's chemical structure) in ways that are quite different from what happens *in vitro* or the drug may have actions on tissues not included in the preparation *in vitro*.

Evaluation of Efficacy *In Vivo*

Evaluation *in vitro* is typically followed by evaluations *in vivo* (in whole living animals). This kind of evaluation includes elements not seen *in vitro* such as extent of absorption from the oral route of administration, persistence in the body, chemical transformation (metabolism) of the administered drug and the potential drug's effects on complex body systems. Because the whole animal is more representative of the human patient, extrapolation to human effects is more reliable, but of course evaluations in whole animals are typically much more time consuming and expensive than *in vitro* evaluations. In addition, ethical concerns may limit the kinds of evaluations that can be done in living animals. Of course, extrapolation of results from animals to humans is often difficult, especially when the therapeutic effect is relatively specific to humans (e.g., effects on mood, thinking, etc.) Nonetheless, as with *in vitro* evaluations, critical evaluation of *in vivo* animal data is key to selection of products with a high chance of successful development. There are a number of concepts that are of use and are summarized in the following sections.

Evaluations of Safety

The requirements for preclinical safety evaluations are elaborated in regulatory guidelines that are readily available on the Internet. One such FDA Guideline is included in Appendix 3. This section will give a brief overview of the requirements for an application to conduct initial human (clinical) trials. More extensive evaluations are required for larger and longer clinical trials, and still more data is required for marketing approval. These additional preclinical studies are described in later parts of this book.

Preclinical safety evaluations are comprised of two types of evaluations: Toxicology and Safety Pharmacology.

Toxicology

Early toxicology studies of new drug candidates should include evaluations for severe toxicity that may make use in humans impossible. These should include evaluations for potential to cause cancer and unacceptable effects on heart rhythm. Mutagenicity testing and hERG studies address these two issues and should be done early in development since they are relatively inexpensive and adverse findings may make successful development impossible independent of any other findings. These are generally supplemented by evaluations designed to detect a wider spectrum of potential toxicity and include general toxicology studies and safety pharmacology studies.

Mutagenicity

Drugs that cause cancer as a side-effect (carcinogenic drugs) are obviously handicapped relative to those that do not. Often, though not always, carcinogenicity is an absolute bar to successful drug development. Fortunately, there are simple techniques that allow quantitation of the risk of carcinogenicity early in development. These include mutagenicity testing, which can be up to 90% accurate in predicting the outcome of more definitive (and time-consuming) studies of carcinogenicity. Mutagenicity testing entails looking for adverse effects on DNA, and is done both *in vitro* and *in vivo* following highly standardized methods detailed in relevant regulatory guidelines. Data from two mutagenicity tests; an Ames test and a chromosomal aberration test should be in hand prior to human exposure. If one or both are positive, additional mutagenicity evaluations should be done.

Computer simulations can also provide an effective screen for compounds with a risk of carcinogenicity. Ultimately, however, long-term studies of carcinogenicity which usually take 3 to 4 years to complete are required for regulatory approval. As I am sure the reader can appreciate, it is important to reduce the probability of an adverse finding in the definitive carcinogenicity studies as much as possible because they will likely be found late in the development process after much time and money have been expended.

As a practical matter, molecules should have: at least 3 negative mutagenicity studies (and no positive tests), no obvious structures known to be associated with carcinogenicity and if possible no evidence of carcinogenic potential based on computer simulations before large clinical trials are initiated. Since these kinds of tests are relatively quick and inexpensive, it is sometimes worth doing them early, for example prior to initiating human trials, since favorable results lower the risk of problems later on. Notwithstanding the foregoing, some carcinogenicity can be tolerated if the expected life span of the patients who will receive the drug is short, due to age or illness. This is because drugs usually take many years to cause cancer, and so, their carcinogenic properties may not be important in patients who will not live long enough to get cancer from drug exposure.

Effects on Cardiac Conduction

Certain effects on cardiac rhythm can pose a large risk to patients and therefore can be a significant or complete impediment to successful drug development. Fortunately, a quick screen for toxic effects on cardiac conduction is available in the hERG assay which should be performed prior to initiation of clinical studies. The hERG assay is performed by exposing tissue that is conducting electrical impulses, to the potential new drug *in vitro* and observing the drug's effects. The test is generally quite predictive of effects on heart rhythm *in vivo*. However as an *in vitro* test, it does not, in general, include an evaluation of effects of metabolites (if any) and this must be kept in mind when evaluating the full risk/benefit ratio of the product.

General Toxicology Evaluations

General toxicology studies are designed to screen for a wide variety of potential adverse effects in animals. Regulations in major developed countries require such evaluations before human testing is initiated. These "toxicology" studies evaluate effects on various organ systems and behavior. Generally, initial studies are conducted to evaluate tolerability in a gross manner, such as effects on body weight, behavior and survival. These early studies are typically used to estimate the doses for later studies to detect more subtle adverse effects. The guidelines for design of these toxicology studies are specified by the International Committee on Harmonization and should be carefully consulted before any toxicology studies are undertaken.

Toxicity is typically evaluated in a rodent and a non-rodent species (usually the dog). Studies included in the regulatory application to conduct human studies should include evaluations of the effects of single doses up to doses that cause significant toxicity or are lethal. This gives insight into the toxicities that can be expected in response to high drug exposure. Such studies typically involve evaluation of obvious behavioral signs and as well as evaluation of lesions observed by gross observation (not using a microscope) on necropsy. The single-dose tests usually don't involve microscopic evaluation of tissues (histopathology) although this can be included if the toxicity observed grossly seems to warrant it.

Once the general ranges of tolerable doses are identified in each species, longer studies must be conducted. These studies should include doses that approach, but do not achieve, lethal doses, so that the non-lethal side-effects can be studied more carefully. Such sub-chronic studies typically include evaluation of histopathology, and organ weights, in addition to gross evaluations and evaluations of effects on behavior, blood chemistries, blood cells, coagulation, etc. These later studies must be conducted according to "Good Laboratory Practice" Guidelines, which specify strict record-keeping and verification of the procedures of the study, including potency of the drug used. In general, the maximum exposure of humans is limited to the duration of the longest toxicology studies which must be carried out in a rodent (usually rat) and non-rodent (usually dog) species.

The toxicity of drugs can sometimes be dependent on the duration of dosing. Thus, it is important to do animal toxicity studies of sufficient duration as early as possible. Typically, studies of at least one month are completed prior to human dosing. However, if there is evidence of cumulative toxicity, longer animal studies are typically justified. Since all effective drugs have toxicity, it is important to be sure that the toxicology testing is done in a way most likely to reveal toxicity as early in the development process as possible. This minimizes the chance that severe toxicity will be seen after a large investment is made in human studies, or worse, that severe toxicity will appear unexpectedly in human studies, which can sometimes be catastrophic. It is critical to objectively contemplate the likely toxic effects related to a drug's mechanism of action and look for them aggressively. These effects are typically exaggerated therapeutic effects whose magnitude is greater than desired but may also be effects that are only indirectly related to the desired effects.

Particular attention should be paid to cumulative toxicity; that is toxicity that worsens with continued dosing. This can be a serious problem for drugs intended for chronic administration to human patients, and it is often a reason to abandon further development. Luckily, most toxicity abates with continued dosing due to the development of tolerance. In such cases, slow upward titration of doses may improve tolerability both in animal and human studies.

It is possible that meaningful adverse data generated in the animal toxicology studies will have to be included in the approved Package Insert and possibly included in promotional material. Therefore, it is important to assess safety information from the skeptical point of view of the healthcare providers who will ultimately read the Package Insert.

Safety Pharmacology

Safety Pharmacology is typically assessed initially by an evaluation of the drug's of effects on a large panel of drug receptor binding assays (to look for unexpected pharmacologic actions). In addition, effects on rodent kidney and pulmonary function, and effects on dog cardiovascular function and behavior are evaluated.

Toxicokinetics

Assessments of blood levels of the drug and its metabolites are typically included in the safety pharmacology and sub-chronic toxicology studies. This is called evaluation of toxicokinetics. These will later be compared with blood levels in human volunteers to assure that the blood levels in the volunteers remain well below levels associated with meaningful toxicity in animals. In addition, the levels of the major drug metabolites should, in general, also be kept below the levels associated with animal toxicity and therefore metabolites should be assessed in the blood of the toxicology animals as well.

Metabolism

Metabolites are typically first assessed using *in vitro* studies of liver cells or cell components from the rodent and non-rodent toxicology species, which are then compared with results from human cells. A qualitative difference between human and animal metabolism may be a reason to consider changing the species used for the toxicology evaluations. Once the main metabolites are identified *in vitro*, they are assayed in blood samples from animals used in the toxicology studies.

The initial human study typically involves assessment of ascending single-doses of the drug, which are generally limited to doses below the levels that cause meaningful toxicity in animals. As mentioned in the "Toxicokinetics" section above, this limitation may be applied to blood levels as well, so that blood levels in humans are kept below those that produce meaningful toxicity in animals. The procedure for doing this is discussed in the following sections. Similarly, the duration of human dosing is generally limited to the longest exposure evaluated in the general toxicology species. Thus, data from both a rodent and a non-rodent species must be available from studies that are at least as long as the longest human study.

Evaluating the Risk/Benefit Ratio

If possible, the comparisons of tolerability should be done in the same animal species and via the same route of administration as were used for the evaluations of efficacy, so that the safety and efficacy results can be compared. The dose with no adverse effect in the most sensitive species used for safety testing is called the "No-Adverse-Effect" level (NOAEL). The ratios of the NOAEL dose in the safety studies to the doses that are effective in the efficacy studies is the animal analog of the therapeutic ratio that will be investigated in human studies, and is often similar in animals and humans. Thus, it is important that this ratio be as high as possible. Anything less than 10 should be considered risky and alternative products with higher ratios should be substituted, if possible. It is also important to evaluate the nature of the efficacy and side-effects because these can affect the tolerance for low ratios. Thus, more severe side effects may be acceptable for a product with potentially unique life-saving efficacy. Similarly, minor side-effects occurring at therapeutic doses may be acceptable when severe or life-threatening side-effects are not.

Once the non-clinical efficacy and safety data are in hand, it is important to have a formal assessment of the risks and benefits of proceeding to human studies. This should include assessments by experts in evaluation of preclinical and human safety data and usually include an assessment by a physician. Warning signs include: low or non-existent margins between doses (and/or blood levels) that are associated with efficacy and unacceptable toxicity. Irreversible toxicity is also a concern especially when the toxic signs are severe or disabling. As mentioned earlier cumulative toxicity that intensifies with continued dosing can be a major problem. All of these concerns should be evaluated objectively with the welfare of the patients and healthy volunteers foremost in mind. A good test is to imagine some completely unexpected adverse outcome from the initial clinical studies and see if the toxicity assessment in hand would seem plausible in retrospect as a justification to grieving relatives or a jury.

Always remember that drug development is research and therefore the outcome is uncertain. Unexpected adverse events do occur and all reasonable efforts to avoid them should be taken prior to initiation of clinical studies.

One might think decisions on the risk/benefit of proceeding to human studies would be relatively simple. In practice, they are often extremely difficult. By the time a complete database of safety and efficacy data are in hand, considerable time and money have been expended. Thus, a decision not to proceed may be very painful to the company and individuals within it. The ability to make this judgment objectively is perhaps one of the most important qualities of a successful drug-development team. Given the low numbers of new drug approvals, it seems that wrong decisions are frequent occurrences.

Chapter 4 - Ethical Concerns and Legal Considerations

General Ethical Considerations

DRUG DEVELOPMENT IS a form of research and as a result, the outcome is inherently uncertain. There is always some level of risk in clinical trials. This risk must be balanced against the potential benefits to the study participants and society in general. In general, the risk of study participation must be balanced by a reasonable expectation of potential benefit to the study participant. However, in certain cases, such as the healthy-volunteer studies to be discussed in the following section, there may be no benefit to the study participants other than the payment they receive as compensation for their participation. In that case, the risk must be held to a minimal level. In general, when there is only financial benefit to the participants the risk of participation should be no greater than the risks associated with ordinary life activities, such as driving to the study center.

Of course, risk can never be completely eliminated and therefore severe adverse events, including death, may occur in spite of the most conscientious efforts to avoid them. Even studies that involve only well-studied drugs still have some risk of allergic reaction, idiosyncratic rare toxicities, and/or adverse psychological consequences to the study participants. This brings up the question of how much effort to reduce risk is reasonable. Criteria are available in the form of regulatory guidance documents that outline what kinds of data are required to support clinical trials. One of these is included in Appendix 3. It is important to remember that these guidances are general and cannot anticipate every new situation, and so the drug development team must carefully review each new drug's potential for toxicity, and address it in the way that lowers the risk for human subjects as much as possible. Thus, especially if the drug candidate has a unique mechanism of action, its physiological effects should be considered both from the point of view of efficacy and safety and the appropriate pre-clinical studies conducted to evaluate potential adverse effects.

Since evaluation of risk to human study participants is very important, the drug laws of most countries require multiple approvals for clinical studies, all of which must be satisfied before a single study participant is enrolled. These include review by the pharmaceutical company sponsoring the study, government regulators, the clinical investigator(s) implementing the study, review by an independent committee of experts ("Institutional Review Committee" in the US and "Ethics Committee" in the EU), and finally, by the study participant.

Naturally, it is important that all the available data be supplied to those evaluating the safety of the study. It is of particular importance that any data suggesting risk be clearly presented in an understandable manner. Data that appears to have been concealed can be very damaging should something go wrong during a study. Conversely, it is valuable to have approval from multiple, fully informed outside bodies in case an unexpected serious problem occurs. The more objective these outside reviews are, the more useful they will be in supporting the reasonableness of a study to the participants and legal authorities and of course on hopefully rare occasions, they can they identify potential problems that the development team misses.

The evaluation by the study participants is done based on an informed consent document which summarizes all the data relevant to their evaluation of the risks and benefits of participation in the study. Since most study participants are not experts in drug development, it is important that the information be presented in words that are understandable to them; avoiding complex technical terms and concepts as much as possible.

These considerations exemplify the required ethical behavior expected by society and required by law and regulation and they also serve as protection for the sponsor if the unexpected should happen.

Special Situations

Certain situations are deserving of special consideration. One such situation is the study of potentially severe or fatal drug effects. In general, studies to rule out the occurrence of potentially severe or fatal adverse events should not be undertaken in humans, unless the potential clinical benefit to the patients is very large. This is because, unless the potential benefit to the study participants is very large, the study, by definition, has an unacceptable risk to benefit ratio. If the study should demonstrate that the drug is associated with a severe or fatal adverse event, then the data will show the number of patients harmed by the medication, and by implication, the number harmed by the investigators and sponsors of the study. This undesirable outcome is likely to be associated with massive finger pointing, blame shifting, litigation and legal fees and is therefore best avoided. If a medication is suspected of being associated with severe toxicity in some patient groups, it is best to just advise such patients to use alternative therapy, rather than risk proving they are harmed by doing a study that injures or kills them.

Recently, a class of popular drugs was suspected of causing rare, severe, or fatal adverse events in a small subgroup of patients. One approach to this risk could have been to advise any patients in the subgroup to avoid the medication. In fact, studies of patients in the high-risk subgroup were undertaken. The studies proved the concerns were real by actually harming and killing patients. The findings caused several of the drugs to be removed from the market, denying them to many patients at very low risk who could probably have benefited from them.

The Forgotten Ethical Issue

Logic dictates that management would always push to develop drugs as quickly as possible, to increase the value of the company's stock, as well as to enhance chances for promotion and financial compensation. Companies do sometimes work this way.

However, the decision to deliberately fail to develop a potentially valuable drug expeditiously is surprisingly common and represents an ethical issue that is rarely considered or addressed in our society. For example, a life-saving drug might not be developed because the potential market is considered too small, or because the product does not fit with the overall direction of the company. In addition, as described above, there are many factors unrelated to commercial success of a product that can delay its development. When, as is general practice, the product is patented, this kind of decision can deprive patients of life-saving therapies for the duration of the patent protection, typically 20 years or more.

When a patented product is known to possess unique and important clinical benefit, the decision not to pursue development or the inability to move development forward expeditiously, represent ethical issues, for they deny society at large an important and possibly life-saving medication. One of my motivations for writing this book is to help companies develop drugs more quickly and inexpensively so that more can enter the development process.

Legal Considerations

Opportunities for making serious mistakes are remarkably common in the drug development business. Serious mistakes may have serious consequences for an individual or an organization. Most mistakes have only financial consequences; for example an individual may be fired or demoted for making a mistake or a company's stock price may fall. However, when a company starts clinical trials, criminal liability becomes a possibility. This is not a completely theoretical issue.

Pharmaceutical company employees have occasionally been jailed for violating the Food and Drug laws. The most common problem occurs when a company does not adequately or expeditiously report new risks to regulators, physicians involved in human studies and people receiving an experimental medication. A general principle is that potential risks and benefits must be accurately and thoroughly communicated to regulators, patients, volunteers, and physicians involved in clinical trials. A key document for communicating risk/benefit information is the "Research Investigators' Brochure." This document must contain a thorough objective summary of all risks and benefits in accordance with a standard format specified in the relevant ICH Guidance Document.

All the non-clinical data should be written up in reports that are thorough and objective. Each report should contain a summary and, if possible, the summary should contain all the information necessary for the relevant section of the Investigators' Brochure. Conforming to these standards from the beginning, makes it much easier to prepare the Brochure once the reports of the individual studies are available.

It is important that the Brochure be complete, fair and balanced. If there are unexpected adverse-event problems during the human studies, regulators, and lawyers will likely be scrutinizing the source documents and Investigators' Brochure for evidence that risks were not accurately portrayed. Failure to accurately portray risks to patients and volunteers is a criminal offense, and therefore the reports and brochure documents will play an important part in the defense against potential civil <u>and criminal liability</u>.

FDA regulations require special procedures when new data suggesting previously unknown risks are obtained during the development process. The new risks must be promptly reported to regulators, clinical investigators conducting clinical trials, the Institutional Review Committees involved in the clinical trials and, in most cases, to patients and healthy volunteers who are receiving or will receive the drug in question. The deadline for reporting depends on the seriousness of the new risk and is specified in the relevant FDA guidance. These deadlines must be met both for ethical reasons and to avoid criminal and civil liability. Since the reporting requirement is an ongoing obligation, newly obtained information must be carefully evaluated for evidence of new risks. It is critical to have adequate human resources (including a licensed physician) and standard operating procedures in place to meet these reporting requirements prior to starting human studies. Often, the first standard operating procedure for the clinical development group covers reporting of safety information.

Chapter 5 - Initial Human Testing: The IND Application and Phase I Studies

The IND Application

BEFORE HUMAN TESTING is started, an application for permission to proceed must be made to and approved by the relevant national regulatory authority. In the United States, this application is called an "Investigational New Drug Application" or IND. In Europe it is called "Clinical Trial Exemption" or CTX. The application contains all the data accumulated in the animal safety and efficacy studies, as well as detailed information about the methods used to manufacture the drug substance and product, and the procedures used to assure their quality. The IND also includes a summary of the human studies planned for the year following the application. It is customary to include a copy of the protocol document for the first planned human study. This protocol specifies in great detail the procedures to be used and the people responsible for various aspects of the study.

The IND also contains a copy of the Research Investigators' Brochure and Informed Consent document that will be used for the first study. The format and content of an IND or CTX application is specified in the relevant regulatory guidance documents.

Once the IND is submitted, the FDA has 30 days to review it. If the FDA issues no objection within the 30-day limit, the planned clinical studies can proceed. Sometimes the FDA will have suggestions for changes in the study or plan that they will communicate during the 30-day review period and these suggestions should be taken seriously since the FDA reviewers frequently have a great deal of experience with other drugs of the same class. Furthermore, as discussed in later sections, it is critical to maintain a collaborative relationship with the FDA and other regulators since they may become very difficult if they feel their concerns are being ignored. If one or more FDA reviewers feels the risks of the human studies are too great, mandatory requirements for changes will be issued. Failure to, or inability to accept these requirements will result in a "Clinical Hold." This means the FDA will not approve the proposed clinical trial, and therefore, no clinical trials may be legally conducted until the FDA is satisfied that they can be conducted safely.

A clinical hold is very undesirable for a company and the FDA. The FDA dislikes them because of past criticisms that the FDA slows the drug development process unnecessarily, and clinical hold statistics have sometimes been used to support such criticisms. A clinical hold is also very bad for a company. This is because there is effectively no deadline for the FDA to resolve a clinical hold. Thus, communications regarding mitigation of the FDA's concerns typically go on for a year or so before the company is allowed to proceed.

In almost all cases, clinical holds can be avoided via a pre-IND meeting with FDA (and/or equivalent meeting with other regulatory authorities). A pre-IND meeting should be scheduled at a time when enough data are in hand to allow a reasonable assessment of the risks and benefits of starting human studies so they can be presented to the FDA reviewers. Such a meeting is preceded by submission of a Briefing Document summarizing key data and highlighting any potential problems or controversial points. It also includes a list of questions for the FDA reviewers to consider. It is far better to clear up any issues before the IND is submitted, even if it takes some extra time, than to suffer the long delays caused by a clinical hold. The pre-IND meeting is also an excellent time to review the entire clinical program and the desired labeling, and get feedback from the FDA before a large investment in clinical trials. The FDA (and other national regulatory agencies) often has very strict constraints on the nature of the indications they will grant. Since the approved indications are critical to the commercial success of a product, it is very important to obtain agreement that the desired indications are acceptable to relevant regulatory agencies.

I cannot over-emphasize the importance of maintaining a collaborative relationship with national regulatory authorities: it speeds the development process many fold and can lower costs dramatically. Because the regulatory meetings are so important, it is critical to have experienced people prepare the Briefing Document and attend the meeting. Every attempt to look at things from the FDA's perspective should be made in advance of the meeting to maximize the chance that they will find the plans acceptable.

Phase I Studies

The main objective of Phase I testing is to evaluate the toxicity profile of the product in humans. The first choice that needs to be made is whether to evaluate the toxicity in healthy volunteers or patients. Healthy volunteers offer the advantage of having relatively few (expected) adverse events so that the toxicity of the new drug can be distinguished most easily from unrelated concomitant events. In addition, because their systems are not compromised by illness, healthy volunteers can often tolerate unexpected toxicity better than patients. Thus, assuming the expected toxicities (based on the animal experiments) are relatively benign, and assuming the doses to be tested are much lower than (by 100-fold or more below) the doses that cause severe or lethal toxicity (not to be confused with the NOAEL which is generally much lower than the minimum lethal dose) in animals, healthy human volunteers are typically used for initial studies.

When meaningful toxicity is expected, there must be some counter-balancing benefit to the phase I participants. Thus, patients who may benefit from the treatment are typically used in this situation. It is important to remember that the risk/benefit ratio must always show minimal net risk, or in the case where the risk is more than minimal, a net benefit for the study participants. Be advised that net benefit to the world at large is not a justification for putting individual patients at more than minimal risk (e.g., the risk of driving to the study site) without a balancing benefit.

The Single, Ascending-Dose Tolerance Study

In order to keep the risk as low as possible, single doses are typically studied first. Orally administered drugs are typically given under fasted conditions, to eliminate potentially confounding effects of food on drug absorption. The first dose studied should be no more than 1/10th the highest dose associated with no adverse effects (NOAEL) in the most sensitive of the animal safety studies. Once the safety of the initial dose level is established, a dose that is double the initial dose can usually be investigated. Then, doses can be repeatedly doubled until unacceptable toxicity is encountered or a dose is reached that should reasonably be expected to have maximal efficacy.

Some researchers recommend that the dose should be increased until significant toxicity is produced, so that the nature of this toxicity can be used to guide the safety evaluations in later clinical studies. While there may be some logic to this approach, in general, it is not necessary to achieve a maximal tolerated dose in humans for both practical and ethical reasons: the toxicity associated with very high doses should have been well characterized in the non-clinical (animal) toxicity studies, and it is not reasonable to produce significant toxicity in healthy volunteers who have no reasonable expectation of benefit from the drug treatment.

At the other end of the spectrum, some researchers recommend that individual volunteers being treated with a new drug for the first time be dosed at wide intervals, so that if unexpected severe toxicity occurs in the first volunteer, dosing the remaining volunteers can be aborted. Although this procedure makes theoretical sense, it is almost never used in practice. The low ratio of human doses to the toxic doses in animals seems to provide enough protection in the vast majority (but not all) of cases.

Although severe toxicity is very rarely encountered in phase I studies, minor adverse events are common. Typically headache, dizziness, nausea, and upper respiratory symptoms are seen because these are commonly seen in untreated healthy populations. In order to help distinguish between drug-related and unrelated adverse events, it is prudent to include a few placebo-treated subjects at each dose level evaluated. A typical study design would include 6 subjects treated with active drug and 2 treated with placebo. The study should be blinded so that the clinical investigator cannot be sure who is on active and who is on placebo.

Once a dose level is completed, it is important to fully evaluate all the safety information before giving the next higher dose. If the pharmacokinetics (blood levels) of the drug are not expected to be linear, (linear means that the blood levels increase in proportion to the dose administered) it is probably prudent to evaluate blood levels for each dose before going higher. This helps assure that the blood levels do not go up by more than double for each increase (generally double) of the dose.

Although usually not feasible, incorporation of evaluations of efficacy parameters should be considered in the phase I studies. These parameters may be the same as those used in definitive studies of efficacy or may be surrogates known to predict the results of more definitive studies. Surrogates should only be used if they are well established to be predictive of clinical efficacy in definitive studies. If no evidence of efficacy is found at maximally well-tolerated doses, then discontinuation of development of the product should be seriously considered.

Following completion of the single-ascending dose study, the blood drug levels achieved at maximally well-tolerated doses should be compared carefully to the levels required to show efficacy in animal studies. If blood levels at maximal well-tolerated doses are lower than blood levels required for efficacy in animal models, then discontinuation of the drug's development should also be seriously considered. One alternative to discontinuation is use of an alternate dose form (for example a delayed release formulation) or alternate dose regimen (for example slowly increasing the dose which can reduce toxicity in some cases).

Some drugs are highly bound to blood cells or blood proteins. Since it is generally the "free" concentration of drug (that is, drug not bound to blood cells or proteins) that determines efficacy, adjustment for binding should be done when comparing results from animal studies, human studies and *in vitro* results, if necessary.

The Multiple-Dose Tolerance Study

Following completion of and evaluation of the data from, the single-ascending dose tolerance study, a multiple-dose tolerance study is typically conducted. This kind of study typically evaluates the effects of dosing over one to two weeks and its design is otherwise similar to that described for the single-ascending dose study. Each dose level would typically evaluate 12 subjects (with four receiving placebo and the remainder receiving active treatment). Again, the tolerability (and blood drug levels, if they are expected to increase non-linearly with dose) are evaluated for each dose before a higher dose is tested.

The starting dose for the multiple-dose study is generally equal to the highest well-tolerated dose identified in the single-ascending dose study. The dose administered in the single-dose study may be administered all at once on each day of the multiple-dose study or it may be divided into lower doses administered at intervals during each day; depending on the drug's blood half-life, as identified in the single-ascending dose study. The dose interval would typically be set based on the half-life of the drug in blood. Usually, one wants to maintain a relatively constant blood level that is at or above the level associated with efficacy. Thus, a dose interval of one to two times the blood half-life is usually appropriate. If the blood half-life exceeds 24 hours, a single daily dose regimen is typically used even though a longer dose interval might also work. This is because dosing at intervals of several days is often difficult to use in patients who may forget doses that are not taken at intervals of at least once-daily.

Following completion of the multiple-dose tolerance study, the blood levels achieved at the maximally well-tolerated dose should be compared with the levels associated with efficacy in animals. If maximally well-tolerated doses do not achieve blood levels associated with efficacy in animal studies, discontinuation of development should be seriously considered, especially in the absence of supportive evidence from any efficacy endpoints that have been evaluated during phase I.

Conversely, achievement of well-tolerated blood levels that exceed those associated with efficacy in animal models and positive results from surrogate marker evaluations are strong support for continued development.

The single and multiple-dose studies are typically followed by an evaluation of the effect of food on tolerability and drug blood levels. This is done so that one can determine if it is necessary to consider limitation of dosing relative to food in later efficacy studies.

Special Evaluation of Cardiac Effects According to Worldwide Mandate

Recently, worldwide regulatory authorities (including the FDA) have become more concerned with effects on cardiac conduction and have mandated a standard evaluation of these effects with a special emphasis on evaluation of certain kinds of electrocardiogram (corrected QT interval) changes. A standard design for such studies has been proposed by the European Medicines Agency (EMEA) and this design should be implemented. Care must be taken to assure quality data collection as outlined in the EMEA Guidance Document.

Substance Testing During Manufacture

The methods used to manufacture the drug substance and product will likely change during development, because larger studies require larger quantities of drug substance and product and the manufacturing equipment and methods will change as production is scaled up. Since each study builds upon the results of earlier work, it is important to be sure that the same product is being tested at each stage of development, and that changes in the manufacturing have not resulted in a change in the performance of the product in humans.

Demonstration of equivalence among the different batches and lots of drug substance and product is typically done using two methods. Dissolution testing evaluates the rate at which the drug product dissolves in simulated gastric and/or intestinal fluid. This kind of testing is used to demonstrate equivalence of products that are manufactured using very similar methods. When larger changes in manufacturing are necessary during development, then bioequivalence between the differing lots needs to be established. This can be done using a bioequivalence study of standard design.

In some cases, changes in the drug substance or product can be made without the need to show equivalence to the prior product. This is true when the new product will completely supplant the prior product, and it is not necessary to use the prior data to support directly the final new drug application. However, it should be remembered that small changes in a drug product or substance can result in large changes of performance, and it can be dangerous to assume that products are the same if the manufacturing methods have changed.

Remember that certain quality standards will apply to a drug product. At the beginning of the development program, it will be impossible to know how well these quality standards are maintained during storage of the drug product. Thus, the quality must be re-evaluated periodically to assure that the product is not changing by a meaningful amount. Each lot of drug product should therefore have an associated "re-test" date when it must be re-tested to assure its continuing quality. Once re-tested, a new re-test date should be established, if appropriate. If the product fails its re-test, it should not be administered to humans.

Setting appropriate re-test dates is very important when planning the longer studies described in the following section. Since a drug product that fails re-testing can no longer be used, re-test failures during a large clinical trial can be a very serious problem, for example, requiring a study to be stopped prior to completion. Conducting larger, longer studies can be very demanding and it is easy to forget to conduct re-testing at the scheduled times. Thus, it is important to have appropriate controls in place to assure that re-testing is done at the scheduled intervals and that studies are not started using drug supplies that are expected to expire prior to completion of the last patient's participation.

Chapter 6 - Phase II Studies

Non-clinical Requirements for Initiation of Phase II

The purpose of Phase II is to establish which doses of the drug show evidence of efficacy and which are too low to show efficacy, and to do a more extensive evaluation of safety than in the Phase I studies. Phase II studies are typically longer and require more patients than Phase I studies. Therefore, more non-clinical information is needed to support the added cost and potential increased risk to the human participants. In particular, data from toxicology studies in a rodent and non-rodent (typically dog) species are generally required to be of equal or greater duration than the planned phase II study (see Appendix 3). These studies must expose the toxicology species to doses and drug blood levels higher than those planned for the phase II study.

It is also prudent to have animal and human metabolism data in hand. This data can be used to assure that the animals used in the toxicology species have been exposed to higher blood metabolite levels than are expected in the phase II study. Obviously, the doses associated with meaningful toxicity in animals should be considerably higher than the levels expected in the planned phase II study. A ratio of greater than 10 between the NOAEL in the most sensitive toxicology species and the highest planned human dose is best; however, this is not a hard and fast rule. At this point the nature and severity of toxic effects should be better understood and used to assure that an acceptable risk/benefit ratio exists.

Design of Phase II Studies

Phase II is the most important stage of drug development, because it is usually the first time it is possible to evaluate both efficacy and safety in humans using standard efficacy parameters. An acceptable efficacy and safety profile is the key to drug approval.

As explained in Chapter 1, a "drug" consists of the actual product as well as its conditions of use. In particular, the dose regimen is a key component of a "drug." Phase I, if properly implemented, should provide the basis for determining the approximate dose regimen that will be both effective (based on blood levels in humans compared with effective levels/concentrations in animal studies) and well-tolerated (based on the side-effect profile seen in the phase I studies). The first phase II study should also include a dose that is considered too low to be effective; including such a low dose should allow determination of a well-defined dose-response relationship when the study is completed with placebo, an ineffective dose, an effective dose, and a higher effective dose, which shows that no greater efficacy is obtained by pushing up the dose. The results at the ineffective dose can be used to answer questions from regulators about whether the doses used in later trials could be lowered to improve tolerability.

This brings up the issue of how to select appropriate doses for phase II. If the doses chosen are too low, no efficacy will be found, and a useful drug may be deemed ineffective. If the doses used are too high, the drug may be deemed too toxic to be useful, and no ineffective dose may be identified. Moreover, the appropriate dose regimen must be selected, e.g., once-daily, twice-daily, etc. The optimal dose regimens should be selected based on the knowledge of drug concentrations known to be effective in animal models and the blood drug levels measured in the phase I studies. In addition, any surrogate endpoint data obtained in phase I should be included in the analysis. I cannot emphasize how important it is to estimate the phase II doses as rigorously as possible. This is because the failure of a phase II study may completely doom a product that would otherwise have great utility.

When phase I studies show that a drug has a short half-life that will necessitate frequent dosing, there will likely be objections that the requirement for frequent dosing throughout the day will make the treatment less convenient, and therefore, limit the potential market for the product. While this is often true, it is important to remember that a failed phase II study will likely eliminate support for further development, dooming the entire project. If frequent dosing is required and is felt to be unacceptable from a patient convenience point of view, the product should be modified so that it can be given less frequently. There are a number of ways of doing this including controlled-release tablet technology and skin-patch formulations. These approaches may also reduce the peaks and valleys of the drug blood concentrations. This often maximizes efficacy and minimizes side effects. Of course if the product is modified in this way, further phase I studies of the modified product will be required before initiation of phase II. Additional, pre-clinical safety studies may also be required to support the phase I and phase II studies of the new formulation. This is especially true if the route of administration is changed (e.g. a patch is substituted for an oral tablet).

Since the proposed dose regimen for phase II is so important, I recommend a formal written justification for the regimen be created and critically reviewed by the team as well as by outside experts. In addition, it is often useful to consult with the team that did the pre-clinical efficacy studies, as they often have special insight into the optimal dose regimen for the phase II study.

The chances of successful development to a commercial product are still small before phase II is completed. Therefore, it is prudent to limit the cost and time dedicated to phase II studies. This can be done by limiting the duration of the patients' participation in the study and using proven surrogate endpoints, rather than the endpoints required for regulatory approval. It is important to balance the cost and time savings achieved using a short duration and/or a surrogate endpoint versus the predictive strength of the phase II study; cost and time savings for a study with little predictive value for the definitive efficacy trials are illusory.

If a long study is required to show evidence of efficacy and no reliable surrogate endpoints are available, then the Phase II study should use the standard duration and endpoints required by regulators to show definitive evidence of efficacy. A low, medium, and high dose should be included with the low dose expected to show limited or no efficacy. This allows demonstration of a good dose-response for efficacy.

If the study can't be shortened or use surrogate endpoints, then the "phase II" study will actually have the same design as a pivotal phase III study (see Chapter 7), and thus could potentially be used as one of the pivotal efficacy studies needed for final marketing approval. When this is done, a company can use a single study to pass two critical steps toward approval, completion of phase II and completion of one of the two required "pivotal" clinical trials.

Since multiple dose levels will generally be evaluated, the issue of statistical adjustment for "multiple comparisons" will need to be addressed. This is discussed further in the next chapter on phase III studies.

Scientific Experts: Advisors and Investigators

The proper design of phase II studies requires detailed knowledge of: (i) the disease state being studied, (ii) concomitant medications that will be used by the study participants including their typical side effects, (iii) the availability of the patient group being contemplated for inclusion in the study, and (iv) many other details affecting study design and implementation.

There are two sources of information that can be used to aid with these practical issues of study design and implementation: clinical investigators and advisors. Investigators who will be considered for participation in the phase II trial, are typically academics who work at large university medical or other clinical centers and make significant income by doing clinical trials for pharmaceutical companies. Scientific advisors are also frequently from the same kind of background. However, they are retained as independent advisors who will not be recruiting or treating patients in a study.

When possible, it is best make the distinction clinical investigators and scientific advisors clear from the beginning. Each brings their own potential set of conflicts of interest, and this should be kept in mind when interpreting their advice. The fact that clinical investigators participate in the conduct of clinical studies means that they have an inherent conflict of interest with a pharmaceutical company that employs them as a scientific advisor on study design and implementation; this is because as a scientific advisor, they stand to profit financially by recommending a study that they (and perhaps only they) can implement. For this reason, scientific advisors should be kept separate from potential investigators who will implement the study. This limits the potential for conflicts of interest. However, even scientific advisors, who are told at the outset that they will not be involved in clinical trials may benefit by directing studies to colleagues with whom they have relationships. In addition, it should be recognized that the academic world is very competitive and scientific advisors may have potential conflicts with one another. For this reason, it is best to meet with scientific advisors one at a time. This minimizes the potential for time wasted with introductions, posturing, and competition for recognition and attention by the advisors. It also reduces the need to resolve scheduling conflicts among advisors who are typically very busy.

It may be impossible to reach absolute consensus on a study design among multiple advisors. If so, it will be up to the company representatives to weigh the various opinions and make a decision.

Scientific advisors and clinical investigators can usually be quickly identified by doing a search of the scientific literature to find who has published extensively in the therapeutic area of interest. Once these authors are identified, they will often recommend colleagues with similar expertise. It is very important to remember that experts often have very limited areas of expertise. One may be very familiar with published literature or basic science but have limited "hands-on" experience implementing studies. Others may be mainly interested in implementation of large studies. Thus, it will typically be important to identify several experts with complementary knowledge in order to assure all areas are covered. These complementary areas of expertise represent another reason to try to discuss issues with each expert separately, so that each discussion can be tailored to the relevant area of expertise rather than asking very busy members of a group to wait until their area of expertise comes up on a meeting agenda. In my experience, this is a common problem in group meetings with scientific advisors.

Regulatory Review of the Proposed Phase II Study

Once the design of the phase II study is settled with outside advisors, it is very important to get input from regulators. As a practical matter, relevant regulators should be contacted and asked to schedule a meeting (I call this an "End-of-Phase I Meeting") as soon as it is clear that a draft phase II protocol can be available in time for the meeting. The FDA will require a Briefing Document for the meeting at least 1 month in advance, and this requirement should be respected absolutely or they may cancel the meeting. The Briefing Document should contain background information on the compound, including a detailed summary of the phase I results, animal efficacy, toxicology and metabolism data and a list of questions the sponsor would like answered. In general, the information should be the same as the Briefing Document for the Pre-IND Meeting updated with the latest available data.

Given the general time limitations of an End of Phase I meeting, the company should have no more than 6 or 8 questions to ask the regulators. While the regulators will usually help with advice, they will generally limit it to answering specific questions. Of course, their advice will only be as good as the information supplied to them, so, it is critical to lay out all concerns and all relevant data in a clear and concise manner. Do not neglect questions about manufacturing of the drug substance or product, for they can be just as important as the design of the phase II study. If significant discussion of manufacturing is required, it should generally be relegated to a separate meeting so there is adequate time to discuss the phase II study.

As previously discussed for the Pre-IND Meeting, any potential risks or problems should be highlighted and discussed openly with regulators. Never conceal information or present it in a biased manner, since it is likely that such a deception will eventually have to be disclosed as development continues and the later it is disclosed, the greater will be the regulator's irritation. In addition, concealing information from regulators is potentially illegal and can lead to both civil and criminal liability.

It is best to limit company attendees to scientific and regulatory experts who can contribute to the scientific and regulatory discussions. Usually no more than 6 or 8 people are necessary. One of the attendees should be tasked to take notes rather than speak since it may be quite difficult for the active participants in the meeting to take comprehensive notes.

Always take regulatory advice to heart. Since regulators cannot compel a company to do things in a particular way unless they feel there is a safety risk, they often temper their language. Even relatively mild qualifications like "we suggest" or "we have found it is best" should be heard as "you had better do it this way or else." Regulators are usually very knowledgeable about the problems occurring in development and their advice should always be taken seriously. If it is not possible to follow their advice, it is best to tell them so as soon as possible and to work out a compromise that they find acceptable. It is almost always a bad idea to disregard the regulators' recommendations without telling them clearly that you intend to do so and hearing what they have to say before you proceed.

Regulators will typically issue minutes following an End-of-Phase I Meeting. Hopefully, these minutes will codify critical agreements between the company and regulators. If the minutes do not clearly address one or more key issues, every effort should be made to get them addressed in writing as quickly as possible in case of personnel or other changes. It is also sometimes possible to get written FDA acceptance of a study protocol through a formal process called a "Special Protocol Assessment." This comes as close as one can to a commitment that the FDA will accept that results of the study if it is implemented as approved.

Implementation of Phase II

The implementation of phase II studies is typically much more challenging than implementation of phase I because the endpoints being assessed are typically more complex to measure than the pharmacokinetic and safety endpoints assessed in phase I. This is especially true for drugs affecting the central nervous system where effects may be based on patient self-reporting and/or subjective evaluations by the clinical investigator.

In addition, phase II studies are typically conducted at sites that mostly deal with patients who are not in clinical trials so they may have less of the infrastructure necessary to collect accurate data. Therefore, it is critically important to have an experienced clinical operations specialist who can evaluate sites for capacity, patient population, and the likely accuracy and integrity of their data.

Phase II studies often require use of more than one investigator site to enroll the required number of patients. When multiple sites are used, a pre-study meeting of the investigators should be scheduled. The conduct of such meetings is discussed in the following chapter.

Although relatively rare, investigator fraud is more common than might be expected, so the clinical-operations specialist must be an excellent judge of character, and must be capable of directing the careful monitoring of the study sites at frequent intervals to assure that the study is properly conducted and the data accurately collected. Obviously, it is best to catch errors as soon as possible, so they may be corrected before they are repeated on more patients. It is important to remember that the clinical investigators will (ideally) implement the study exactly as specified by the study protocol, and anything left ambiguous will likely be done differently at each site, so ambiguity should be scrupulously avoided. Every detail of the enrollment requirements and exclusions, and the study procedures should be included in the protocol, including contact telephone numbers for company personnel, sample collection and shipping procedures for samples and study documents, etc.

Political and Business Considerations

Successfully completing a phase II study by demonstrating efficacy in humans is a pivotal step in the drug development process and if accomplished successfully, it adds a great deal of value to the product. While this is very beneficial for the company that owns the product, it is also the point at which competition over control of the project increases. Everyone wants to be involved with a winner, and if possible, to be in charge. The increase in value that is so essential to the company, often brings out the worst in the personalities involved. Skilled drug-development personnel must have a plan in place to defend their leadership positions or they will often find that new, more "professional" people are suddenly put in charge. These new people may be only skilled political operatives with poor drug development skills and/or impaired ethical principles, who can cause problems when they try to implement the remainder of the development program.

It is the responsibility of upper management to defend the positions of the people who have successfully navigated through phase II. Allowing them to be pushed aside sends a powerful message throughout the company, that superior performance is not rewarded. This can be a fatal message for a company whose future often depends on high performance of its technical personnel. Conversely, the next step, phase III is more demanding than phase II so it is critical to be sure the development team is adequate to the task.

Chapter 7 - Phase III Human Studies

Decision Point - Pressures and Considerations

THE DECISION TO enter phase III clinical trials is perhaps the most fateful of the development process. Phase III is usually much more expensive and time consuming than the earlier phases. In addition, it is usually advisable to initiate final metabolism studies, final long-term toxicology studies, (including carcinogenicity studies, if required) and any remaining phase I type studies (for example, drug interaction studies) prior to, or in parallel with, phase III.

Phase III trials are designed to demonstrate the safety and efficacy of the product in large numbers of patients using the efficacy endpoints accepted by regulators as definitive. Since the trials are designed to show the safety and efficacy of the product to be marketed, it is important that the drug substance and product be representative of the final product proposed for marketing. Thus, many expensive manufacturing activities will be required prior to the start of and in parallel with phase III. Of course all of the data accumulated prior to initiation of phase III should have been obtained using product that is representative of what will ultimately be marketed. So, adequate studies must be done to assure that the product lots used in all the studies will be acceptable to support approval of the marketed product. Special attention should be given to impurities and degradants. These must all be kept at levels which assure the safety of the study participants, but must also be kept at levels greater than or equal to those expected in the marketed product.

Because of the large commitment typically required for a rational phase III program, it is critical that the decision to proceed be made as carefully as possible. The decision-making process should typically include an End-of-Phase II Meeting with the FDA (and equivalent meetings with other relevant regulatory bodies). The objective of this meeting is to verify that the FDA will allow the phase III program to proceed and to confirm that if successful, the FDA agrees the studies will support a marketing approval. Of course, it is absolutely critical to get the proposed protocol approved in writing and this can be accomplished by the Special Protocol Assessment process, previously mentioned (see Regulatory Review of Proposed Phase II study, above).

The decision process for starting phase III studies is neither for the faint hearted nor for the reckless. A careful evaluation of accumulated data and careful statistical power calculations for the phase III studies should be undertaken before the decision to proceed. The following section outlines the key regulatory and scientific considerations that need to be addressed prior to the start of phase III.

Requirements for Initiation of Phase III

It is of great value to have successful phase II data available prior to initiating phase III. These data should confirm that the mechanism of action found in animal studies is applicable in humans. If possible, pharmacodynamic endpoints that verify the non-clinical mechanism of action should be in hand at the end of phase II. In addition, it is of great value to include the standard evaluations required for final FDA approval in phase II. Doing so can provide supplementary evidence of efficacy (even if not statistically significant), and can also provide an evaluation of the variability of the endpoints that must be used in phase III. The effect size (the difference in clinical response between active drug and placebo patients) and variability of the efficacy results found in phase II can then be used for statistical power calculations for the phase III studies. Estimates from actual data are often more valuable than data from published reports of other trials which may not be reflective of typical or current conditions or reflective of the skill of the development team charged with conducting the phase III studies.

Power calculations deserve special attention. These relate to the number of patients required in order to have a reasonable chance of success. The results of power calculations are usually expressed as the percent chance of success assuming the drug works as expected. It is normal to use studies that have 80 to 90% power. This means the studies have a 10 to 20% chance of failing even if the drug works as expected. Power calculations are based on the expected "effect size" (for example the magnitude of the difference between active drug and placebo) and the variability of the efficacy data. It is absolutely critical to use realistic conservative assumptions. For example because the studies are larger, phase III data tend to be more variable than data from phase II studies. The power of the phase III trials should be estimated using a realistic synthesis of data from earlier studies which used the same methods that will be used in phase III. Data from both successful and unsuccessful studies should be used for power calculations to avoid bias.

One might ask why studies are powered only to 80 or 90%. Why not 99%? The answer is that studies powered to 99% would typically require more patients than are practical. Pressure to hold down costs usually translates into pressure to modify the assumptions used in power calculations so that smaller studies can be justified. As mentioned above, typical phase III studies have a 10 to 20% chance of failure even if the drug works as expected. If studies are underpowered, the chance for failure can quickly become much higher. Such failures are especially tragic, because they often lead to discontinuation of a drug from development, even though it would have been shown to be effective if evaluated in an adequately powered study.

It should be noted in passing that the investment community often puts particular emphasis on the start of phase III trials, quoting statistics that show a large proportion of products that enter phase III are ultimately approved for marketing (Booth, Glassman & Ma, 2003, Nature Reviews Drug Discovery 2:609). However, these statistics are, to my mind, suspect. I have seen many companies' products fail during phase III. Statistics are valuable only in the context of the data set they were obtained from. I doubt that the high success rates often cited by the investment community are drawn from a database of products that were inappropriately advanced to phase III based on inadequate data. Conversely, in my experience, a well-supported and well-implemented phase III program rarely fails to supply data that will support product approval. Personally, I have never had a completed phase III study fail.

Since essentially all other development components are timed to conclude around the time the phase III studies complete, a failure in phase III comes after almost all development costs (in time and money) are complete; thus, the critical importance of adequate and conservative power calculations. The head of the development team must often balance the risks of taking a stand for adequately powered studies against the threat from others in the company who will try to replace him or her by claiming they can conduct adequate studies for less money. Although money should never be squandered on over-powered studies, it should always be remembered that the most expensive study is the study that is unsuccessful.

The phase III program will expose many more patients to the drug for longer periods of time than the phase II program and therefore more preclinical safety data is required before phase III begins.

Preclinical requirements needed for starting phase III include the following:

- Toxicology data from a rodent and non-rodent species, with a duration of dosing generally at least as long as the planned phase III trials. Doses must provide a reasonable "exposure multiple" as expressed by dose per body surface area and exposure to blood levels of parent drug and metabolites. The exposure multiple is the ratio between the NOAEL in the most sensitive toxicology species and the highest dose to be given to humans. The acceptable safety margin will depend on the nature of the toxicity found in the animal species: the more serious the toxicity, the greater the safety margin must be. Giving humans doses that are toxic in animals is generally not acceptable, unless the toxicity observed in the animals is very mild, and any more severe animal toxicity occurs at much higher doses than those to be used in humans (See also, Appendix 3).

- Because the exposure in the toxicology studies must be known for both the parent drug and its metabolites, the metabolites must have been identified and quantitated in blood, urine, and feces in the toxicology species as well as in humans. This generally means that studies of the fate of drug must be conducted in both the toxicology species and humans prior to the initiation of longer term toxicology studies. Such studies are often most easily done using drug that has been "radiolabled" with a radioactive atom to make the metabolites easier to detect. Keep in mind that special studies of the distribution and elimination of radiolabel must be conducted in animals prior to the initiation of human radio-labeled studies; therefore, these studies must be carefully planned out so that the results are available at the appropriate times. Lack of adequate data on metabolites is a common impediment to the start of later stage clinical trials, because metabolites are a rather esoteric subject that may be ignored by financial analysts and, therefore, may be de-emphasized when pleasing them is a primary company objective. If possible, metabolism should be assessed in time to have adequate data to support initiation of phase III on time.

- Most drugs that are given chronically require evaluations of carcinogenicity in rodents before they can be approved for marketing. The doses for the carcinogenicity studies must be carefully chosen, so that they maximize the exposure of the toxicology species while not unduly shortening their life-span. A standard set of dose-ranging studies is recommended by relevant regulatory guidances. Once the dose-ranging data are in hand, the proposed design and doses for the carcinogenicity studies should be submitted for formal approval by the FDA. Once an approved design is in hand, it should not be changed without prior consultation with the FDA. In general, carcinogenicity studies can be conducted in parallel with phase III. However, if two or more mutagenicity studies are positive, there is an increased risk of a positive carcinogenicity result. For most drugs, evidence of carcinogenicity is an absolute bar to successful regulatory approval. Therefore when two or more mutagenicity studies are positive, earlier initiation of carcinogenicity studies should be considered to avoid a positive carcinogenicity result after a large investment has been made in phase III studies.

The following table summarizes some key requirements for starting phase III in tabular form.

Category	Requirements	Additional Considerations
Drug Substance	Final drug substance manufacturing process	The drug substance used in the phase III studies must contain the same or lower levels of impurities and degradants as the the drug substance used in the longer-term toxicology studies to support the safety of the phase III studies
Drug Product	Final drug product manufacturing process	The drug product used in the phase III studies must contain the same or lower levels of impurities and degradants as the drug substance or product used in the longer term toxicology studies to support the safety of the phase III studies
Metabolism	The major metabolites and routes of metabolism and excretion in the toxicology species and humans must be known prior to the initiation of phase III	Human and animal radio-labeled drug studies are typically required. Adequate time must be allotted for the synthesis of radio-labeled drug and for the conduct of animal metabolism studies and the animal radio-label distribution studies required to support human radio-label studies.
Toxicology	Results of toxicology studies, generally with a duration at least as long as the planned phase III studies are required in both a rodent and non-rodent species. Exposure to the parent and metabolites must show an adequate safety margin relative to the proposed phase III doses	In order to assure adequate exposure to metabolites, in the longer term toxicology studies, early evaluation of the metabolism in animals and humans should be undertaken. If radio-label studies are required, adequate time should be allotted for the synthesis of radio-labeled drug and for the studies required to support a human radio-label study.
Phase I	The safety and pharmacokinetics of the doses proposed for phase II should have been fully evaluated in single and multiple-dose phase I studies. Careful evaluation of the effects of food and concomitant medications should be in hand to allow adequate instructions for drug administration in the phase III trials. Patients will need to be told if there are potential drug interactions with products they might be taking as well as if food affects the absorption of the investigational product. Evaluation of food effects should include evaluation of the effect of a standard meal on blood drug/metabolite levels. The design of such studies are specified in relevant regulatory guidelines. Effects of specific foods that are known to affect drug metabolism (e.g. grapefruit juice) may also be required.	

Category	Requirements	Additional Considerations
Phase II	Clear evidence should be in hand confirming that the mechanism of action observed in animals is observed in humans. Sufficient data regarding tolerability and efficacy of a number of different dose regimens should be available to support the dose regimen to be evaluated in phase III trials.	
Carcinogenicity Studies	Start these or they won't be available in time for the NDA submission.	The design for these studies should be approved by the FDA before they are initiated. Do not change the approved design without advance approval from the FDA.

Implementation of Phase III Studies

As the most expensive and time-consuming part of drug development, implementation of phase III requires as much care as can be marshaled, at a stage when the pressure to move expeditiously is very high. With the NDA submission now in sight, management is more likely to supply the resources needed to proceed; however, with resources allocated, they will expect rapid progress. This tension between speed and care is a central theme of phase III clinical development. The development team's refrain, "Do you want it now, or do you want it right?" is particularly apropos. Of course, the management's response may be "I am paying for both."

Precautions for Implementation of Phase III Studies

The most important part of a phase III study is the design of the protocol. It must balance scientific rigor against the practical considerations of implementation in the real world. The ultimate validation of the protocol comes from reviews by appropriate governmental regulatory bodies (the FDA in the US). Their approval of a specific protocol should always be obtained prior to implementation of a phase III study. If significant changes are made after the regulators' review, approval of the revised protocol should be obtained prior to implementation.

It is also absolutely essential to have the final drug substance and product available for use in the phase III studies. These must be essentially the same as the product that will be marketed. The degrees of variation are specified in relevant regulatory guidance documents. When in doubt, it is always wise to ask the appropriate regulatory bodies for their approval of any manufacturing changes before they are implemented.

Key elements of a phase III clinical protocol are listed below

- Patient enrollment and exclusion criteria
  o As a general rule, the enrollment and exclusion criteria should result in a patient group that is representative of the patients who will receive the product when it is marketed.
  o Enrollment criteria should be carefully considered because they will affect the scope of the ultimate regulatory approval. The regulatory approval will, in general apply only to the patients studied. Of utmost importance is the definition of the "disease state" because regulatory approval can generally only be obtained for disease states recognized as such by the regulators and there are many "conditions" that regulators don't recognize and for which approvals cannot be obtained. Once an accepted disease state has been identified, it is critical that well-recognized diagnostic criteria be used to set the conditions patients must satisfy in order to qualify for study enrollment including disease staging (e.g. mild, moderate, and/or

severe). Patient enrollment and exclusion criteria should be specified in the study protocol document in a way that facilitates patient recruitment while clearly meeting generally-recognized diagnostic criteria.

o Exclusion criteria can also affect the scope of regulatory approval, and therefore, should be carefully considered and approved by appropriate regulators prior to implementation. Patients with concomitant illnesses or concomitant drug therapy whose data will confuse the analysis of the study data should be excluded, if possible. Conversely, patients with concomitant illnesses or who are receiving concomitant therapies that will be common among the patients who will receive the drug when marketed should be included in the study, if possible.

• Efficacy Endpoints

o These are generally specified by regulatory guidelines, however, regulators will sometimes accept endpoints not listed in the current versions of guidelines. This can happen when new endpoints gain credibility after the guideline is issued or when FDA makes policy changes that affect efficacy endpoints. For example, FDA would not accept effects on "activities of daily living scales" for many years because they believed such scales did not have widespread acceptance in the scientific community. However, FDA has now begun to accept some activities of daily living scales as evidence of efficacy. It is critical to gain approval of the study endpoints from regulators in key countries where the product will be marketed.

o To assure the statistical validity of the study, the primary efficacy endpoint(s) and the primary database should also be clearly identified in the protocol (all patients enrolled, all completed patients, all patients who followed the study protocol, etc.). In general, regulators require the primary analysis to include evaluation of data from all patients with baseline and endpoint values for the primary efficacy variables. If a patient drops out of the study early, his or her last efficacy assessment is used. If a patient receives the wrong treatment (hopefully this never happens), then the assigned treatment, rather than the actual treatment, is used in the primary data analysis. This is called the "Last Observation Carried Forward, Intension-to-Treat" (LOCF-ITT) analysis.

- Safety Assessments
  o These should include standard physical examinations, ECG, laboratory assessments, plus any additional safety assessments dictated by the pharmacology of the product. Again, it is critical to gain approval of the safety assessments to be used from key regulators, since once the study is completed, it will be difficult or impossible to obtain additional safety data without repeating the entire study.
  o The study protocol should include specific instructions on when safety information should be elicited from the patients. In general, patients should be questioned in a general way about changes of their health since the prior visit. Additional questions regarding adverse events identified in earlier studies of the product should be added as appropriate.
- Control Therapies
  o In general, regulators require placebo controls to demonstrate efficacy. Uncontrolled studies are rarely

acceptable, even when the regulators seem to be willing to accept them during initial discussions. So, deviations from general best practices should be confirmed in writing with regulators before a study begins. Initiation of uncontrolled phase III studies should not be undertaken as a basis for drug approval without the utmost due diligence. In the case of serious conditions with currently approved therapies, an active drug can be used as the comparator. Again, this must be worked out with key regulators in advance of study implementation. (see gancyclovir Case History in Chapter 18)

- Population Pharmacokinetics
  o It has recently become popular to collect blood samples for assay of drug levels in phase III trials. Although it is usually not possible to control the time after dosing when the blood samples are obtained, the results of the assays can be interpreted using population-pharmacokinetic analysis. This kind of analysis, if implemented properly, can give information about the effects of various factors (e.g., sex, race, concomitant therapies, etc.) on drug blood levels. It is also sometimes possible to associate adverse events with particular ranges of blood levels which can help practitioners when they use the product after approval.

- Blinding
  o In general, blinded comparator studies are required for regulatory approval. Unblinded studies should be relied upon only after extremely careful validation by regulators in advance. It is important to implement adequate controls to assure the study blind is not broken prematurely due to an uneven distribution of adverse events or through

misadministration of the study protocol (including packaging, dose titration, etc.). A method for emergency unblinding of individual patients by their investigators should be provided in case this information is urgently needed to treat the patient; however, emergency unblinding is almost never needed in practice and can degrade the credibility of the study results if implemented more than rarely.

- Practical Problems of Study Implementation
    o Good Clinical Practice Guidelines require that investigators be trained to implement the study by the study sponsor. This is typically done at a large "Investigator Meeting" where the study sponsor reviews the study procedures such as those in the bullet points above, as well as more generic concerns such as shipment of study samples, obtaining Ethical Committee approval, filing of regulatory forms, etc. It is critical have a well-organized Investigator Meeting run in a professional manner and to mitigate, as much as reasonable, the natural tendency for attendees to concentrate on the recreational activities typically available at the meeting site.
    o Selection of investigators is especially important and should be handled by very experienced site evaluators.
    o Study sites should be carefully monitored (as required by Good Clinical Practices Guidelines) by experienced and well-trained and managed study monitors. This is especially important at the beginning of the study, when correction of mistakes at a site may prevent them being repeated for additional patients.

- Study Timing
    - The end of study will be determined by the duration of each patient's participation and the date the last patient is enrolled. Thus, efforts should be made to carefully monitor enrollment as the study proceeds and to reallocate patients to sites that can enroll patients quickly. Any lag of enrollment should be identified as early as possible, so that appropriate actions (increasing advertising budgets, etc.) can be taken early on when they will have the greatest impact. Loosening enrollment or exclusion criteria or enrollment of patients who do not strictly meet the criteria are often suggested as an aid to enrollment. Loosening criteria should be avoided if at all possible since doing so could invalidate the results of the study. If a change in enrollment criteria is contemplated, one should confirm that the change is within the boundaries approved by the regulators when they reviewed the study protocol. Enrollment of patients who do not meet the protocol-specified criteria should almost never be allowed since this is a violation of the protocol and often a violation of Good Clinical Practice regulations and can therefore, be illegal.

Investigator Meeting

An investigator meeting is required for all studies, and for large phase III trials the meeting must take place at a venue capable of handling the investigators and clinic staff for all sites. The investigator meeting is often critical to the successful implementation of the study. It is very important to use staff who are experienced in organizing and implementing investigator meetings. A meeting-organizing company is often needed to arrange travel schedules and handle reimbursement of expenses, and to assure that the mechanics of the meeting presentations go as planned.

The investigators' meeting should be well organized and cover all the aspects necessary for successful implementation of the study. The protocol and case report form must be in final form prior to the meeting and should reflect feedback from critical investigators.

The attendees should include the staff who will actually implement the study at the various study sites in addition to the clinical investigator who will supervise them. Both groups should be strongly encouraged to attend the relevant sessions of the meeting. Those who do not should probably not be allowed to implement the study.

The meeting should cover all aspects of the study including efficacy and safety evaluations, methods for collection, processing and shipment of laboratory samples, and methods for central evaluations (ECG, MRI, etc.). Most large pivotal studies employ a central laboratory to assure that the normal ranges for lab values are the same for all sites. While this complicates the handling of samples which must be shipped offsite, it simplifies the analysis of laboratory data. In addition, most central laboratories will report receipt of samples for each patient and study visit on a real-time basis facilitating tracking of patient enrollment and progress through the study.

It is critical to assure that the investigators and their staff understand how to fill out the case report forms properly; never underestimate the ability of sites to misunderstand protocol procedures and methods for recording their results when they are not clearly communicated by the development team. It is useful to assure that the development team has communicated effectively by testing the performance of the attendees during the meeting and retraining any personnel whose performance falls outside acceptable limits.

There are usually investigators who question the study design and procedures during the investigator meeting. Although it is important to consider these suggestions carefully, modifications made during the investigator meeting generally represent a failure in preparation by the development team. These late changes often have unintended consequences, since they are made after power calculations are complete, budgets negotiated, discussions with regulators completed, etc.

The last activity of the meeting should be some relatively inviting recreation. This will provide an incentive for the investigators and their staff to remain for the full duration of the meeting and allow them to meet company staff in an informal setting.

After the Meeting

Once the investigator meeting is over, the sites can be initiated by a visit from a study monitor and, provided all required regulatory documents have been filed, shipment of clinical drug supplies. It is useful to monitor study sites early, after enrollment of its first few patients, to assure that the data are being collected and recorded appropriately. These initial visits should concentrate on critical safety and efficacy parameters.

As the initial data comes in, it can be analyzed without unblinding to assure that: the assumptions about data variability are approximately correct, the distribution of baseline patient data is consistent with the power calculations used to justify the study and that the enrollment rates are acceptable.

Note that the variability of the data for a study can often be estimated before the study is completed by conducting the analysis specified by the study protocol but without unblinding the treatments. This calculation will not give any information about how the treatments differ (that will need to wait until the study is completed and the treatment codes are unblinded). However, statisticians can calculate the "standard deviation" of the measurement(s) of primary interest to confirm that they are not more variable (and therefore difficult to measure) than expected. Although these calculations will be only approximate, they may suggest that the study is under or over powered and that the number of patients to be enrolled should be adjusted accordingly. As a practical matter, it would be unusual to adjust the number of patients downward based on this kind of assessment, since a downward adjustment increases the possibility of failure do to lack of statistical power. However, it is relatively common to increase the number of patients based on this type of calculation.

Enrollment is often a problem, being slower in reality than predicted by the sites before the study started. This can often be avoided by discounting each site's predicted enrollment rates based on experience implementing other studies and by collecting recruitment data for each site's prior studies. When, in spite of these precautions, enrollment lags, a number of solutions can be considered: increased site advertising budgets, increased per-patient reimbursements for the sites and/or patients, and as a final resort, increasing the number of sites. When the number of sites is increased, costs for starting them will be incurred and may include sponsoring a new investigator meeting.

Monitoring of safety data during phase III is obviously very important since it is possible that uncommon toxicities will be detected in phase III because the studies involve larger numbers of patients. It is very important to keep on top of the safety information as the phase III studies progress so that any indication of a new risk to patients can be quickly identified and communicated to regulators, investigators, institutional review committees, ethics committees and when appropriate to study participants. Initial safety reports from phase III studies are often vague and provide little indication of the outcome of adverse events. I cannot emphasize how important it is to follow up incomplete reports to assure the patients receive the appropriate treatment and diagnostic procedures (including autopsy, when appropriate) so that maximal information is available for all meaningful adverse events. Since a few occurrences of certain adverse events are sufficient to completely block approval of a new drug application (e.g. death, cancer, blindness, etc.) it is very important to be sure that the report of each serious adverse event is complete and includes risk factors that were present prior to exposure to the drug, concomitant medications or conditions that could be related to the serious adverse event and most importantly, the outcome (recovery, permanent disability, death, etc.). Any missing information about a serious adverse event will likely be interpreted by regulators in the most unfavorable manner so ambiguities should be resolved as completely as possible. The follow-up information should be pursued vigorously at the time of the original report as it becomes harder to get follow-up information as time from the event passes by. For adverse events that are very serious, a small imbalance between the active and placebo group can raise serious problems for approval of a new drug application. Thus, it is very important to obtain as complete a database as possible so small imbalances that may occur by chance can be explained when the full unblinded database is obtained at the end of the study.

Frequently, the full NDA safety database contains more patients who were exposed to active drug than patients exposed to placebo. For this reason there are often more patients with adverse events in the drug treated group than in the placebo group. When an event is rare, it may occur only in the drug-treated group by chance. In such a case it can often be very important to have detailed information that shows why the event was observed. For example, an NDA database may contain twice as many patients in the active drug treated group as in the placebo group. There may be two patients in the active-drug-treated group who had heart attacks. Since there are twice as many patients in this group than in the placebo group, one would expect a single placebo treated patient to have a heart attack if the heart attacks were occurring by chance. But of course in any particular database, there may or may not be a single patient with a heart attack. If a particular database has no patients with heart attacks in the placebo group and two patients in the active-drug treated group, there will be a difference in the prevalence of heart attacks between the two groups with the placebo group having a prevalence of 0%. This can make the active treatment appear to be more dangerous than the placebo treatment with its 0% prevalence. Of course it is possible to state that the difference could be due to chance. However, the regulators, with no way to be sure, may ask for further proof that the difference really is due to chance. In such cases it may be very important to elicit a history of a heart attack, chest pain, high blood pressure, smoking, etc. prior to treatment with the experimental drug. Such histories can sometimes be missed at the time of enrollment in a study and may be critical to approval of a new drug application in some cases.

Phase III Extension Studies

Regulators often require longer duration of exposure (typically up to one year) than will be evaluated in the double-blind pivotal phase III studies. The longer duration of exposure is not typically required for all phase III patients and can often be obtained by adding an extension study that allows patients who complete the controlled phase III studies to continue open-label treatment with active drug for an additional time to give the total exposure required by the regulators. If the pivotal trials have a placebo control, an extension study can offer an opportunity for patients who unknowingly received placebo during the pivotal study to have access to treatment with active drug during the extension and this can help recruit patients who might otherwise not want to enroll in a study where they might never receive active treatment. The object of a longer term extension study is to show that the pattern of adverse events seen does not get worse as time goes by and therefore the analysis of the data should be tailored to address cumulative toxicity.

If an extension study is used to augment enrollment by allowing placebo-treated patients to get active drug, the number of patients enrolled in the extension may exceed the regulatory requirements for long-term patient exposure since this number is usually much less than the total number of patients who receive active treatment in the double-blind phase. In this case, an interim analysis of the partially completed extension study may be adequate for the application to market the product (New Drug Application, NDA), and the remainder of the data from the extension study can often be submitted when it is available. These details should, of course, be worked out with relevant regulatory bodies, well in advance of submission of the NDA.

Chapter 8 - Late Stage Activities

THE PHASE III trials typically require at least one and a half years to implement, analyze, and commit to written reports. During this period all other parts of the new drug application (NDA) must also be completed.

Manufacturing

During the conduct of phase III, the final manufacturing activities needed for the NDA must be completed. This typically involves synthesis of 3 large-scale batches of drug substance and three large-scale batches of each strength of drug product. The drug product batches should contain at least 10% of the number of doses that are intended to be produced in each commercial batch. For a major product, each large-scale batch would contain at least 100,000 or more doses.

It is best if these batches can be used for the actual phase III studies. If this is not possible, the NDA batches must have the same or lower levels of impurities and degradants than the amounts in the batches used for the clinical trials, so that the commercial product can be considered to be of the same or higher quality compared with the product used in the studies in the NDA application.

An NDA typically requires at least 6 to 9 months of stability data for both the drug substance and product in the same containers that will be used commercially. Production must be carefully timed: it must be completed early enough so that carefully monitored data supporting an adequate shelf-life (potency, impurities and degradants must remain within acceptable levels) are available at the time the NDA is to be submitted. Yet, the production of the large-scale batches is expensive and so they should not be manufactured until the investment can be justified based on estimates of the risk-reward ratio for the phase III studies.

A more complete, discussion of manufacturing issues is included in Appendix 3.

Non-clinical

Final toxicology studies are completed during phase III, and they should be carefully monitored to determine whether they produce data that could suggest a new risk to the patients being studied in phase III. The toxicology data should also be reviewed carefully to assure that there is adequate evaluation of all metabolites, impurities and degradants. The oncogenicity studies should be monitored for signs of problems. As discussed in prior sections, evidence of carcinogenicity at this stage of development can be a disaster, as it often may absolutely preclude regulatory approval. Furthermore, if evidence of carcinogenicity is found, all the people who were exposed to the product will likely have to be notified and offered follow-up because they may be at risk of developing cancer.

Detection of active drug in plasma samples obtained from placebo animals is a surprisingly common problem in carcinogenicity studies. This should be carefully looked for during the early parts of the study, and if found, dealt with decisively. Usually, the cause is contamination of the samples after collection and this can be ameliorated by careful collection of samples which should be done as scrupulously as possible. However, contamination can occur via transfer of active drug from one animal to another through excreta or handling. Of course, exposure of the placebo animals to systemic levels of active drug will generally invalidate the study, so, if this happens, a new study should be started as quickly as possible. A new study will also be required if the source of contamination cannot be identified; this is a very dangerous situation since the problem may recur if its cause is not found.

Biopharmaceutics

The main biopharmaceutics tasks that need to be conducted in parallel with phase III involve assuring that the formulations used during the earlier stages of development are the same as those used in phase III and the same as those to be marketed. The methods used to synthesize the drug substance (active ingredient) and to manufacture the final drug product will usually change significantly during the development process. This is because the suppliers for the ingredients may change based on cost or availability, and because different methods are required as the quantities increase to support larger and larger studies. The company (and government regulators) need to be concerned that the data included in the NDA will be representative of the product proposed for marketing even though the methods of manufacture may change significantly. Biopharmaceutics studies are designed to address this issue; whenever there is a doubt about the comparability of the formulations, bioequivalence should be assessed and hopefully, confirmed. As long as the regulatory bioequivalence criteria are met and there are no differences in degradants or impurities in the formulation, there should be no problems supporting the NDA.

Clinical Pharmacology

By the time the phase III studies are completed, all clinical pharmacology studies should be completed. These should typically include: all the phase I tolerance studies, demonstration of the relationship between dose and blood levels, characterization of metabolism (including a study utilizing radio-labeled drug), evaluation of the effect of renal and hepatic disease on drug levels, and any additional studies that may be needed to understand how the product should be used or promoted. Specifically, it may be useful to do additional drug interaction studies which may not be absolutely necessary but which may provide data to augment dosing recommendations in the product Package Insert.

Integrating Late Stage Activities

As the phase III studies near completion, there will be a great deal of activity aimed at integrating the data obtained during the earlier development process with the data being obtained from Phase III. This includes confirming that stability, degradants, and impurities are the same for products used in critical safety evaluations (clinical and non-clinical), and assuring that no new safety problems can be identified. Any drug interactions identified should be analyzed as appropriate and any safety issues identified during the blinded part of the phase III studies should be carefully followed up so that adequate supporting data are available at the time of the NDA submission.

It is also possible to begin preparing the reports of the phase III studies. Although the results will, of course, not be available, the methods sections can be drafted and an outline of the other sections can be prepared. This shortens the time to prepare the NDA later on.

Since many of the activities at this stage require a comprehensive and detailed knowledge of the data obtained during the entire development program (often accumulated over a number of years and in many countries), it is very important to try to keep the development team intact and functioning efficiently.

Breaking the Blind and Final Steps

Although it is impossible to assure the outcome of the efficacy evaluations in phase III studies, if they are properly designed, implemented and analyzed, they should be successful from the efficacy point of view in most cases. Since power calculations are typically done to give an 80% to 90% probability of being successful, there will theoretically be a 10% to 20% chance that the study will fail by chance (because of bad luck), even though the product is effective. In reality, power calculations should be based on conservative assumptions so that the study's real power is much greater than predicted; this assures that the studies will show efficacy in the large majority of cases. It is also possible to increase the chances of success of the entire phase III program by implementing three or more phase III studies in case one fails due to bad luck. If the failed study comes close to being successful, then it shouldn't be an impediment to approval of the NDA. Negative studies are frequent for certain indications, e.g. depression, Alzheimer's disease, so more than two phase III studies are often conducted in parallel for these indications.

If properly designed and implemented, the major risk of phase III studies should be finding rare serious side-effects that generally could not be detected in smaller trials. Certain signs of rare toxicity can sometimes be inferred from small studies. However, sporadic severe toxicity can occur without this kind of warning. This kind of sporadic rare toxicity represents a risk that cannot be completely eliminated prior to completion of the phase III studies and breaking of the study codes.

It is critical to collect all the study data, carefully review it for inconsistencies and missing data, and resolve all issues before the study code is broken. Critical study populations should be identified in writing (e.g. patients in the LOCF-ITT, per protocol and safety databases and their critical endpoint values). This maximizes the quality and credibility of the study data, and thereby maximizes the chance of a successful NDA approval. There will, of course, be pressure from management and perhaps investors to break the blind as soon as possible. However, it is important not to impair the credibility of the results by breaking the code prematurely.

Once phase III studies have been successfully completed, the great majority of the time and expense of drug development have past. This is no time to ruin the compound's chances for successful regulatory approval through careless mistakes so care in implementing the development process must be elevated to the highest possible level.

Well before completion of dosing of the last patient, plans for collecting and entering the data should be finished. The data collection process consists of a number of steps:

1. Entry of the data on the protocol case report forms for each patient
2. Review of case report form data by the company's study monitor
3. Resolution of all inconsistencies on the case report form
4. Signature of the case report form by the clinical investigator
5. Shipment of the signed case report forms to the data entry site
6. Entry of the case report form data into the study database
7. Computerized data consistency checks and generation of data queries designed to resolve apparent inconsistencies
8. Shipment of the queries to the study site and study monitor
9. Resolution of the queries
10. Modification of the case report form and computer database to reflect resolution of queries

Many, and in some cases all of the above steps can be done electronically, saving paper and time. The case report form may also be broken down into modules for each visit which can then be processed as the visits complete. This speeds the data entry and analysis process.

It is imperative to keep in mind that the steps listed above must be conducted in compliance with Good Clinical Practice Guidelines to avoid any appearance that inaccurate data are being inserted in to the study database. Thus, the reason for any change should be clearly documented, and the name of the person authorizing the change should be recorded, along with the date the change is made. Dating is particularly important because there is a great difference between changing the study database before, rather than after the double-blind code is broken. Obviously, every effort must be made to avoid changing the data after the code is broken to avoid the appearance that bias has been introduced.

In addition to locking the database, it is critical to be sure that the statistical methods to be used in the data analysis are specified in detail before the code is broken. This is typically done by issuing a Statistical Plan prior to the code break, and ideally, prior to the implementation of the study. This statistical plan should be reviewed and approved by FDA prior to the code break. It is critical that the Statistical Plan document be dated so that it is clear that it was finalized prior to the code break.

It is often difficult to adhere to the procedures outlined above because there is intense pressure to complete the study and find out the results as quickly as possible. These must be balanced against the risk of a premature code-break, since a mistake can result in a failed NDA. It goes without stating that this stage of development requires experienced, strong management from the project team and concerned support from upper management.

The work and stress leading up to the breaking of the blind usually is so draining that it is not possible to have much of a celebration if the studies are successful. This is especially so because press releases typically have to be drafted, and work on the NDA must be expedited.

Political and Business Considerations

The period during phase III and especially after successful completion of phase III represents an even larger value creation point than the corresponding periods for phase II. Thus, many people will be competing to replace and/or augment the people in the development team. As is the case during earlier stages of development, it is critical that management support the development team in the face of what will often be self-serving criticism from less successful groups within the company. If unwarranted changes are made in the face of outstanding performance, not only will the development process be endangered, but also, a powerful negative message will propagate through the company affecting the development of other products. On the other hand, management must assure that the development team has adequate support at this critical time; this means the team should be encouraged to engage whatever help they deem necessary (within reason) without fear that a request for support will result in a loss of authority or credit. This can often be accomplished via use of outside consultants, so long as they are used in a way that does not disrupt the functions of the team.

As described in the prior section, completion of the study reports required for the NDA can involve many steps. A delay of any step may delay completion of the study report. The delay of a single study report (the NDA will typically contain dozens) will usually delay the entire NDA submission. Therefore, is it very important to closely track the detailed status of each report to assure that they are all progressing as scheduled and that nothing is delaying progress along the planned critical path.

An important part of managing the end of phase III is preserving confidentiality, so as to avoid the possibility of misuse of the phase III results for stock trading. Thus, documentation of steps taken to preserve confidentiality should be done very carefully, and all reasonable steps to encrypt confidential information should be used.

Chapter 9 - A Word on Phase IV Studies

O NCE SUCCESSFUL COMPLETION of phase III is in sight, it is important to consider what additional data are necessary to support marketing of the commercial product. Such studies need to be scientifically valid, but they do not necessarily need to meet regulatory approval criteria. In certain cases, regulators may require phase IV studies as a condition for acceptance or approval of an NDA application.

Often marketing-oriented people will be involved in the selection and/or design of phase IV studies. They may neglect the potential impact of a negative phase IV study and therefore it is critical that phase IV studies be evaluated by people capable or weighing the probability and potential impacts of all the possible study outcomes.

A rule of thumb: Don't investigate questions unless you can accept all the realistically possible answers. For example, do not undertake a study designed to show your drug is superior to a competitor unless you are very sure that the study will validate your hypothesis of superiority. Also, it is generally not a good idea to evaluate drug effects on endpoints that are not well accepted by the scientific community because even if the results of the study of such endpoints show the desired effect, they may be interpreted in a negative way by some members of the scientific community.

This is not to say that studies should be biased so as not to obtain negative results. All studies should be aimed at gathering data that will aid healthcare practitioners when they use the product. This may sometimes involve characterizing patient groups who should not receive the product because of undue risk; although this may initially reduce the market for the product, it will likely reduce the chances of serious problems during marketing, thus contributing to the long-term success of the product. I believe there are a number of approved products that ended up being removed from the market because they were used by inappropriate patient groups.

Chapter 10 - NDA Submission and The NDA Submission Team

NDA Submission Team

AS DISCUSSED MORE completely in the following sections, creating a successful NDA involves integrating a vast database of biopharmaceutic, clinical pharmacology, metabolism, safety, efficacy, and manufacturing information. The NDA must unite these disparate parts into an easily-understandable, consistent whole. Every bit of information collected must be included in the NDA; yet, the summaries must be simple enough for a harried FDA reviewer to easily understand. This is no mean feat, and a critical aspect of accomplishing it is to preserve the team that supervised the development process and to keep it highly motivated to create a successful NDA application.

One might think that changing the team at such a late date is unusual. However, I have seen it occur or almost occur on a number of occasions.

Pre-NDA Meeting

The format and content of an NDA submission are specified in the relevant FDA Guidance Documents (and the European equivalents). However, each FDA division has different preferences and may require additional analyses beyond those in the Guidance Document. It is, therefore, an excellent idea to request a Pre-NDA meeting with the relevant FDA division once the results for all the NDA studies are in hand. This is an important opportunity to gain the FDA's acceptance that the data look adequate for approval (subject to review of the full data during the NDA review process) and to find out what formats the Division wants for required computer files. Although a sponsor is not required by law to go beyond the Guidance requirements, it is in the sponsor's interest to provide any support the FDA requires to facilitate its review and these requirements are best gleaned through a well planned pre-NDA meeting. It is important to be forthright about any potentially controversial issues during the meeting. This will allow FDA to explain what they think they need to address the issue efficiently, and this will speed the review process. Hiding issues will typically result in requests for the needed analyses during the NDA review which may delay the review significantly, as the harried FDA reviewers put aside the NDA application while waiting for the requested analyses. During this period, they may busy themselves reviewing a competitor's application. Minutes are typically issued following a Pre-NDA meeting. These are important mostly because they help the development team prepare the NDA in a manner that will be most efficient for FDA to review.

Since the format for a marketing approval application (MAA, the EU equivalent of an NDA) is somewhat different from the requirements in the US, pre-NDA meetings with EU regulators are recommended.

General Considerations for Presenting NDA Data

NDA documents should present data in a fair and objective manner. This allows the FDA reviewers to use parts of the NDA documents verbatim in their review, saving them time and resulting in a quicker approval. Conversely, attempting to hide or minimize adverse findings can cause the reviewer to check the application in greater detail, greatly slowing the approval process. I caution sponsors to avoid trying to fool the FDA reviewers. Not only is this potentially illegal, it is extremely unlikely to be successful.

It is impossible to exaggerate the care with which reviewers evaluate NDA data. Since the reviewers have a limited ability to check the accuracy of the data submitted, they instead focus on evaluating its consistency. Thus, it is absolutely critical to assure that the data presentations are consistent; every patient who enters a study must be accounted for and their data included. If data are missing, this must be clearly indicated. The results of every blood assay must be included and summarized, and all the patient numbers, sample numbers, efficacy results, etc. must be carefully checked for consistency. Regulators take a very dim view of incomplete or inconsistent presentations and, as discussed below, inconsistencies can result in delays or rejection of an NDA application.

NDA Documents

In large part, an NDA consists of individual study reports and summaries that integrate their results. Reports are typically thousands of pages long. For the FDA, summaries may be dozens or hundreds of pages long. (For the EU, summaries are typically limited to a few dozen pages called "Expert Reports." However, these relatively brief summaries are often supplemented with much longer appendices.) In total, an NDA usually consists of hundreds of thousands words in tens of thousands of pages bound in dozens of volumes. It usually requires a modest size truck to deliver an NDA to a regulatory body.

Key summaries include the following:

- Chemistry and Manufacturing – This section includes information about manufacture of the drug substance and product and their stability during storage. The US, EU and Japan have differing standards for inactive ingredients so this section will differ slightly for each territory.
- Non-clinical – The format for summaries of non-clinical data can vary between countries. Thus, adequate time and personnel must be allocated to the task of making up the proper summaries for each territory.
- Biopharmaceutics – This summary should include the results of all studies relevant to the blood levels produced by different batches of the drug product. Specialized tables are required for the NDA, including various details of each study's design and results. The format of these summary tables varies in different countries, so they usually need to be done separately for each region of the world (Asia, EU, and the USA).
- Clinical Pharmacology – This summary is often a duplicate of the Biopharmaceutics Summary, since there is often a

great deal of overlap between clinical pharmacology and biopharmaceutics studies.

- Clinical Efficacy Studies – These are typically the last studies to be completed and their reports are generally very long with numerous appendices. It is critical to assure that adequately experienced and trained personnel are allocated to the task of completing them.

Since the NDA summaries cannot be completed until the reports of the individual studies are completed, the summaries are frequently on the critical path to the NDA approval. Thus, it is advantageous to format the study reports to minimize the work required to generate the necessary NDA summaries; since each report will typically include a separate study summary, it is useful to format the study summaries so they can be lifted verbatim into the NDA summaries. It is also important to try to assure as much consistency as possible among the individual reports. Typical inconsistencies include:

1. Use of different drug names; generic versus brand, internal company code, chemical name and various abbreviations.
2. Use of different methods of expressing drug potency; e.g. free base or acid versus salt. Regulators generally require use of the free base or acid, when applicable, so this should be used from the beginning, if possible.
3. Use of different pharmacokinetic parameters or units making comparisons across studies difficult (e,g, AUC_{o-t}, AUC_{o-24}, AUC_{o-inf}, ng/ml, nM, etc.) This should be standardized from the very beginning of the development program.

As each study report is completed, the relevant section of the NDA summary can be quickly generated. When the last report is completed and its summary inserted into the relevant NDA summary, it is tempting to declare the summary complete; however, it is critical to take the time to have the summaries reviewed as a whole to eliminate inconsistencies between the different summaries, and to be sure that all issues that could affect the safety and efficacy profile of the drug are adequately addressed. The regulators will ultimately be concerned with clearly elucidating the safety and efficacy profile of the whole NDA application rather than study by study.

It is wise to present a coherent, balanced analysis that the regulators can use in their reviews verbatim. This will speed the regulatory review process and minimize the chances for surprises during the review process. Also, as mentioned previously, misrepresentation of the results of studies can result in civil or criminal liability.

The final steps in preparing an NDA include binding the application documents in volumes, numbering each of the volumes and all pages and packing the NDA for shipment. It is also typical to prepare an Adobe Acrobat® version of the NDA. This will involve joining all the Acrobat files for the individual documents and providing the appropriate cross-links between the tables of contents and the text and between the different sections of the text. Although preparing this Acrobat file is not unduly complicated, the work is typically time consuming, and adequate personnel and time should be allocated to this task. Usually, the FDA will allow the Acrobat file to be submitted somewhat later than the paper version of the NDA. It is likely that the FDA will dispense with requiring the paper version and that only Acrobat files will be allowed at some time in the relatively near future.

NDAs are of sufficiently high value that it is worthwhile to have them shipped to regulatory agencies by special courier. It is often useful to send a regulatory affairs professional along to assure there are no problems with delivery.

Most regulatory bodies now require payment for their reviews. The amount to be paid and mechanics of submitting payment often change, so, the details should be confirmed with the regulators just prior to submission. At the time this book was written the FDA cost for a new molecular entity was $896,200.

Chapter 11 - The NDA Review Process

FDA REGULATIONS REQUIRE a through review of the submitted data. Many of the key calculations will be replicated and verified by the FDA, and source data will often be reconciled with the summaries provided by the sponsor. Since a typical NDA contains hundreds of thousands, or millions, of words and numbers, it is inevitable that apparent discrepancies will be noted by FDA. These apparent discrepancies will be sent to the sponsor in the form of questions or requests for clarification. It is very important the discrepancies be apparent and not real. Any meaningful error in the NDA will probably stimulate a more detailed and time-consuming review, causing delays that are a problem for both the FDA and the sponsor. When questions arise, it is important to answer them as quickly as possible and a one-day turnaround time is a good objective to shoot for. Responses should rarely take more than a few days. As noted above, FDA reviewers are pressed for time, and a delayed response will often cause them to shift their attention to the review of another sponsor's application.

During the review process, the FDA will also send inspectors to key investigator sites. Therefore, it is critical to assure that all sites have well organized and easily available records. It is also a good idea to have a sponsor's representative present prior to, and during, the inspection to assure that records are provided in an efficient and courteous manner.

The FDA will also likely inspect the plants proposed to manufacture the drug substance and marketed product. Therefore, every effort should be made to assure that records are well organized and readily available. A regulatory affairs professional should be available at the time of the inspection.

Regulatory inspections are discussed more completely in Chapter 14.

Chapter 12 - The Challenges of Success

THE ULTIMATE VALUE creation point for the development team is the completion and submission of the NDA, and ultimately, NDA approval. At this point the visibility of the development team is maximal, and therefore, the competitive juices of other groups within the company will likewise be maximal. It is critical for upper management to resist the inevitable criticisms that will flow from less successful personnel and to provide lavish rewards to the successful development team. These should be in the form of monetary compensation, promotions, and assignment to high-profile new development projects.

Unfortunately, this often does not happen. Instead, there is great pressure from the less productive personnel to minimize recognition of the successful group. This is especially true when an NDA is submitted by a small subsidiary distant from the centers of management powers. Pressures of various types will often be brought to bear as, for example, pressures to implement large deviations from the procedure used for the successful NDA. This is done in the hope that members of the successful development team will refuse and can be fired for insubordination, or even better, will resign.

At the time when these pressures are most extreme, employment opportunities for the development team also increase substantially. Developing a drug successfully is quite unusual, and the team members will be courted by companies that want to get their own drugs successfully developed. The best strategy for the development team is to hang on until fired with severance pay; getting a new job is usually quickly accomplished and the severance pay will substitute for the bonus that is insufficient or is not granted for a successful NDA approval.

Losing a successful development team is often catastrophic for the company over the long run. However, this long-term problem is often obscured for years, since the revenues from the newly launched product will divert attention from the fact that no new products are being successfully developed. In the meantime, the members of the development team will typically have flourished in new, more hospitable surroundings.

To those unfamiliar with the pharmaceutical industry, it seems incredible that a successful drug development team would be fired just after the drug is approved. However, I have observed it myself on numerous occasions and all concerned should be prepared to deal with it. Talented drug developers tend to replicate to repeat their success at their new companies, while the company losing the development team often has difficulty getting more NDA approvals. I believe this movement of talented personnel from one company to another is why the pharmaceutical industry will remain relatively fragmented, with no single company able to dominate success in the drug approval process.

Chapter 13 - Types of New Drug Applications: 505b1, 505b2 and 505j NDAs

THE DEVELOPMENT PROCESS outlined in the prior section is applicable to new chemical entities, that is, products containing active ingredients never before approved to be administered to humans. The FDA refers to this type of NDA as a "505b1" application after the applicable section of the Food, Drug and Cosmetic Act.

Generic products do not have to include all of the data discussed in the previous sections. Typically, generic products are approved based on submission of manufacturing and blood drug (and if applicable, metabolite) levels alone. The remainder of the required data is accessed through reference to data already on file at FDA from another sponsor's submission. Generic products are approved under section 505j of the Food Drug and Cosmetic Act.

The Food Drug and Cosmetic Act also allows approval of products that fall between pure generics and new chemical entities under section 505b2. This section covers new forms and new combinations of previously marketed drugs. For example, a new formulation (liquid instead of tablet, controlled-release instead of immediate-release, etc.), or a combination of two drugs previously marketed individually, would typically be approved under Section 505b2.

Given the dearth of new molecular entities, many companies have turned to developing new combinations of products that are already marketed. Many of the considerations outlined in the preceding sections also apply to development of new combination products. However, combinations are also covered by the FDA "Combination Policy", which requires proof that all components of the combination product contribute to its efficacy. Thus for a product containing components "A" and "B" a study would need to be done to show that the "A+B" combination is more efficacious than either A or B given alone. In addition, it is often necessary to show that all the active treatments are superior to placebo. This necessitates a four-arm study comparing placebo, A, B, and A+B. It is usually more difficult to show differences between active treatments than to show differences between active and placebo. Since the combination study often needs to show both, it can be challenging to implement successfully.

A shorter path to approval for a combination drug can sometimes be taken. If a drug is already approved for use in combination with another drug for the same indication, then it is often possible to obtain approval for a combination tablet containing both active ingredients in a single-dose form based on blood drug level data. The logic is that the combination therapy has already been shown to be useful, so all that needs to be demonstrated is that the new combination-dose form produces the same blood levels as the individual dose forms that are already approved. This approach has been used successfully for a number of products.

Chapter 14 - Inspections by Regulatory Agencies

REGULATORS MAY CHOOSE to inspect any facility (manufacturing, office locations, investigator sites, etc.) at any time; with or without advance notice. Typically, scheduled inspections will occur prior to an NDA approval and will include inspections of the clinical sites that enrolled larger numbers of patients and the manufacturing facilities. Usually, the FDA will notify a company of the date of the scheduled inspection so there is time to prepare. This time should be used for practice inspections to get the staff used to the procedures that will be followed during the real inspection.

In addition, unscheduled inspections can occur at any time. The inspection manuals used by FDA are publicly available documents, and they should be referred to for preparation. It is important to remember that when an FDA inspector asks for a document, it must be supplied within a few minutes or it will be considered not to exist. It is of course very important to be courteous and helpful to the inspector.

There are a few items that FDA inspectors are not entitled to inspect and it is sometimes important to draw the line and politely refuse to produce them in the unlikely event that they are requested by an inexperienced inspector. However, full cooperation is the most advisable course, if possible.

The objectives of an FDA inspection will vary, depending on the facility and type of inspection, and the details are too complex to discuss here. In general, inspections seek to confirm that a company is following relevant laws and regulations regarding the safety and quality of their experimental and/or marketed products, and that acceptable tracking systems and records are maintained so that this can be confirmed by both the company and the FDA.

If the company is doing a good job, the results of the inspection will generally be a powerful confirmation of the quality of work and record keeping.

At the end of the inspection, the inspector will meet with company representatives to report his or her findings. At this point, the company has a final opportunity to explain apparent discrepancies or omissions. However, as mentioned above, it is generally too late to produce new documents. Once the inspection is over, the FDA will issue a final inspection report.

Management should be acutely aware of the results of inspections and action should always be taken to address deficiencies, no matter how trivial they may seem. The actions taken should be documented, so that the company can prove it takes suggestions for improvement seriously. Actions taken to deal with apparent problems should also be communicated in writing to FDA. This is a good message to FDA, employees, and to the public. The public may become involved since the results of the inspection often become public information.

Clinical sites may be the subject of a regulatory inspection and all study protocols should inform the investigators of this possibility and require them to notify the company of impending inspections, so that a company representative can visit before hand to make sure all appropriate records are easily available. The company representative should be present during the inspection assure that the site personnel are cooperative and that appropriate corrective action is taken, if necessary.

Employees often complain to their management that the results of an inspection are unfair. Such complaints are easy to make since the inspector will not be available to present the FDA's point of view. In my experience, it is always appropriate to take the results of an inspection seriously. As discussed above, even when the deficiencies cited are very trivial, take the time to correct them, document the correction, and inform FDA of the actions taken. In addition to proving to the FDA and to the public that the company is responsible, it also can be very important in case of litigation. A company's first job is to do quality work; however, doing quality work may not be enough if it can't be effectively communicated to regulatory bodies through evidence of proper record keeping and communication with regulators. If the regulators are perceived as being unreasonable (as they occasionally are), their concerns must be either allayed or appealed. Allaying their concerns is usually the most efficient route and most likely to be successful. When a regulator makes a mistake, it should be corrected using discretion; for example, it is often unwise to point out the mistake when the regulator's supervisor is present. If the error is blatant, try to put a good face on it. Regulators are people too and, if possible, it is desirable to maintain a positive collaborative relationship.

Establishment inspection reports available on the FDA website and through Freedom of Information requests and are a very valuable window into the functioning of a company. Yet the public and the investment community are often unaware that this information is available. Repeated problems cited in inspection reports can result in punitive actions by FDA. For example, the FDA may force closure of a manufacturing facility that may be the only source of an important product(s). FDA can also refuse to review new marketing applications from a company with repeated violations found during inspections. Clinical data from an investigational site may be invalidated and excluded from analysis if problems are found at the site even if the problems do not affect the quality of the data collected. For example, failure to get adequate informed consent from patients can result in disqualification of data from a site, even though all other parts of the study were conducted in an acceptable or exemplary manner. Losing data from a site can cause a study to fail, making a product unapprovable.

Significant and/or repeated problems with regulatory inspections is almost always an indication of severe problems with company management and indicative of adverse long-term prospects.

Chapter 15 - Rules of Thumb and Other "Tricks of the Trade"

Evaluation of Personnel

IN THE DRUG development business, getting the proper people is key to success, so this is perhaps management's most important task. The best predictor of future performance is past performance. Be sure to hire people who have specific, hands-on experience successfully performing the tasks you will require of them. The pharmaceutical industry is filled with people who were on committees, have had only a peripheral connection to the drug that received approval during their tenure or have only very high level management experience with little experience handling the multitude of issues that are critical to successful drug development. If you can't ask detailed questions, find someone who can to assist with the interview process. Be sure that the person assisting you will not be threatened by the hiring of other very capable people.

Evaluation of Companies

Most companies have great difficulty developing drugs efficiently, therefore, it is critical to confirm a company's ability to do drug development before accepting an offer of employment. This can usually be done quite simply by checking to see how many drugs they have been able to get approved in the recent past. A good source will be the company's annual report. If it is long on promises and short on actual approvals, beware. In addition, the results of FDA inspections of companies are usually publicly available and are a very useful guide to the inner workings of a company by an objective independent source. Serious or recurrent inspection problems are a significant warning sign that management is not performing well and that long term, this will impact the company's profitability.

Evaluation of Contract Research Organizations

Contract research organizations ("CROs) are companies that will conduct some or all of a development program on a contract basis. Their capabilities vary greatly and so they must be selected very carefully. The CRO business was once quite profitable; however, like many businesses based mostly on repetition of relatively simple tasks, its profitability has been hurt by increasing competition. This has resulted in pressure to employ less qualified staff and to use pressure tactics to obtain payments. Thus, any CRO contract should contain strong language protecting the sponsor from staff changes and from billing increases once a large project is started and it is hard to switch to a new contractor. It is also important to check references and reputations and to assure that the size of the project is adequate to keep the CRO motivated to do a good job. Specific, successful, recent experience in the therapeutic area of interest should be an important part of the evaluation of a CRO.

In no case should strategic issues be decided by a CRO. They have an inherent conflict of interest and can often recommend studies that only they can do or that are unnecessary, in order to inflate their revenues.

Regulatory Approval Documents

One of the quickest ways to learn about what it takes to get a new drug approved is to see what was successful for someone else. Fortunately, the FDA and the EMEA make some of their reviews of new products public. Most are available on their websites and often give details about the review process that are highly instructive for the drug development professional as well as for potential investors.

Knowledge of what was required for prior products allows one to estimate what will be required for a new product enabling better planning, and more informed negotiations with regulatory bodies. Relevant approval documents should always be reviewed and thoroughly understood prior to embarking on any development program. They should also be carefully reviewed prior to meetings with regulators. This is because regulators are heavily influenced by precedents set by prior approvals and are understandably cautious about deviating from what was required in the past because of potential criticism for making arbitrary decisions, and because any deviation from past practices may set a new undesired precedent.

Reviewing regulatory approval documents can also be very helpful to potential investors, since they provide a reality check against plans and claims made by companies about the regulatory hurdles they face.

FDA Advisory Committee Meetings

Whenever the FDA is faced with a decision they don't want to make on their own, they will convene a panel of outside independent experts, an Advisory Committee, to review the issues involved and make a recommendation. Advisory Committees are standing committees available for the FDA to use when they feel it is necessary. In the past, FDA usually requested input from advisory committees during the approval process for every new drug. However, with the recent pressures to approve drugs more quickly, the committees have been used less. One can only speculate as to why an advisory committee will be asked to participate in the review of one product and not another. However, it appears that there are three main reasons FDA uses a committee meeting as part of the review process:

- FDA may be genuinely unsure whether a product should be approved. This is typically the case for a very novel compound for which there is little or no precedent.
- FDA is under significant political or public pressure to approve a product that they feel has an unfavorable safety-efficacy profile. In such instances, the Advisory Committee provides political cover for what FDA feels will be an unpopular decision.
- The approval of a product will set a new precedent that FDA will likely be pressured into following for future products. In this circumstance FDA will often want to get concurrence of the Advisory Committee before proceeding.

An FDA advisory committee meeting to review a new drug application is typically public and anyone can attend for free. An agenda and list issues to be resolved is made public, usually a day prior to the meeting. On the day of the meeting, the company/sponsor's representative(s) will typically present the company's interpretation of the data first. This is followed by FDA's interpretation presented by relevant FDA staff. The members of the Advisory Committee usually have many questions both for the company and FDA representatives. Finally, the advisory committee attempts to answer the questions posed in advance by FDA, which typically require "yes or "no" responses, by majority vote.

Since the FDA usually follows the recommendations of the Advisory Committee, and the committee will usually be asked to recommend for or against approval of a product for each of its proposed indications, the outcome of the meeting is very important to the company/sponsor. Thus, a company should spend as much time and effort preparing for the meeting as is required to ensure that its representatives will be prepared to answer every question that comes up, definitively and expeditiously. It is also sometimes helpful to enlist the support of recognized scientific experts from outside the company if they can help support the company's point of view.

Attending an FDA advisory committee meeting is the fastest way to learn about the how companies interact with FDA. There is a very wide spectrum of performance: some companies are truly magnificent at presenting compelling scientific evidence in a clear and concise manner; some companies will present thin support for their product or may rely mostly on emotional appeals from desperate patients; some companies may resort to criticism of FDA as unfair, unreasonable or worst of all untruthful. Arguments that involve direct criticism of the FDA usually receive a cool reception from the Advisory Committee members and result in a vote for rejection of the marketing application.

This book can't describe the value of watching the FDA and company presenters in action during an advisory committee meeting. The emotional tension and performance of individuals under fire is fascinating to watch and highly educational. Sometimes the health of vast numbers of patients and billions of dollars hang in the balance and the eb and flow of a product's fortunes are more fascinating to me than any other kind of entertainment.

It is a shame that more of the public does not get to see advisory committee meetings. I think the American public would have a much better understanding of the challenges that face FDA and a better appreciation of the generally superb job they do at regulating the drug industry if these meetings were available via the Internet or cable TV.

I would recommend periodic attendance at FDA advisory committee meetings to anyone seriously interested in the pharmaceutical industry, including financial analysts, development professionals, and non-scientific managers. It is one of the quickest and cheapest ways to learn about the practical aspects of drug development other than reading this book. And it's great entertainment.

Costs and Timelines

Much has been said about the costs of bringing a new drugs to market. The major drug companies and their trade association quote figures close to a billion dollars for each new drug developed. This very high cost is used to justify the high costs of prescription drugs. My guess is that the very high figure is calculated by totaling annual research and development costs and dividing them by the number of new drugs approved each year. According to this definition, the costs of each new drug are indeed very high. If this calculation method was really accepted, there would be very few drugs worth developing.

However, the calculation is heavily influenced by the cost of the very high level of expensive failures during development. The actual cost of doing the studies required to get one new drug approved is much lower. For a new chemical entity, a cost between $45 and $70 million dollars is typically adequate. Another $10 million or so may be spent on additional studies that are not required for approval but may be needed to support promotion of a new product. Indeed, studies designed to support marketing of a product may be much more expensive than the studies required for approval, especially because they continue for the much longer period while the product is being marketed. The expense of getting a new product approved (up to $70 million) may be compared to the typical first year marketing budget for a new product, which is often in the range of $200 million. Thus, it is clear that much of the cost of a new drug is associated with promotion and marketing rather than the cost of studies required for approval.

As mentioned previously, the cost of failed programs typically comprise the majority of research and development costs. Thus, the extreme importance of limiting the cost of programs that are destined to fail by devising strategies that identify them at an early stage. My team has been quite successful at this. We have never had a program fail in phase III because we always sought to design small, relatively inexpensive phase II studies that identified programs that were very likely to succeed, and more importantly, programs likely to fail.

It is interesting to note that the cost of actually manufacturing most drug products is remarkably low, typically about $0.03 per tablet, including packaging and labeling. Thus, the cost of most prescription drugs reflect the costs of marketing, failed development and profit. The cost of successful development programs is minor by comparison.

A typical new chemical entity development program should take no more than 5 or 6 years from the first study in humans to the new drug application (NDA). Companies that cannot adhere to this kind of schedule should be suspect.

FDA review of a new chemical entity should take no more than 10 months. At the 10-month time-point, a complete response letter will typically be issued. Complete response letters are quite variable. In most cases the complete response letter should state that the FDA is willing to approve the product if the company sponsor will accept the proposed Package Insert text included in the letter. This text is usually subject to some negotiation between the FDA and sponsor, which should take no more than one or two months. In many cases however, a complete response letter will include additional requirements or pre-conditions for approval. These may be simple to respond to, or they may require very expensive and time-consuming work. When there are extensive requirements for additional work in the complete response letter, it is an indication of a severe failure by the development team, since any serious problems with the NDA should have been identified and addressed much earlier. This kind of problem should be regarded seriously by management and investors.

The Value of Being Second to Market

It is always exciting to think of being the first to market with a new important therapy. The concept has great power for both development personnel and the investment community and certainly novel, first-of-a-kind therapies can be very successful. However, it is important to be realistic about the challenges of bringing a truly novel product through the development process. For example, there will likely be no directly applicable regulatory guidelines that can be used to outline the design of a clinical development program acceptable to key regulatory bodies. This means there must be even greater emphasis on frequent interactions with regulators, so that any change in their positions can be included in the development plan. As mentioned previously, all effective therapies have some toxicity and for a novel agent, the toxicities will likely be novel as well. This will mean that additional safety data will be required to assure that a rare serious adverse event will not be missed. Thus, regulators will likely require larger numbers of patients and longer durations of exposure for truly novel agents.

Every development program will have several unexplained adverse events in both the animal and human studies. For agents with well known mechanisms of action, it will be easier to dismiss such events as random findings that occur any time a large number of observations are made. For very novel agents, more follow-up work will be required, including repeating studies to see if the "rare" events recur and turn out not to be as rare as they initially appeared.

The extra challenges involved in developing a truly novel agent often make it reasonable or even desirable to be the number-two product in development. The sponsor of the first product to reach the regulators will have to negotiate all the criteria for approval, size of safety database, etc. with the regulators; the company coming second will have a much clearer understanding of the requirements for approval, likely adverse events, etc. This often makes planning and implementing development much more efficient, so that the time between the approval of the first and second products may be much shorter than expected.

My informal experience is that the second product to be approved often comes to dominate the market place. This was true for the H_2 antagonist anti-peptic ulcer drugs and for the drugs used to treat Alzheimer's disease, among others.

Being number two can also be the only viable strategy for a small company. If the company with the most advanced product is skillful at dealing with regulatory challenges, it will blaze the development trail in a way that a small company might find difficult or impossible. Just such a situation occurred during the development of a proton-pump inhibitor drug that is discussed in Chapter 18.

Managers of small companies developing novel compounds should keep in mind the extra difficulties that can be expected and not be unduly discouraged if a larger organization appears to be pulling ahead in the development process. Investors should be aware of the extra risk of failure or delay involved in the development of a truly novel new drug.

Development of Products Already Approved in Other Countries

Although drug development is an increasingly global activity, the approval process is still done country by country. Thus, many products are approved for sale in only one or a few countries. In some cases this may be appropriate if the indication is limited to a particular region (e.g., malaria). However, most illnesses are global in nature, and therefore a product with a good market in one country has a much better chance of successful development in another country than does a product that has never been approved.

Complications arise with respect to patent protection in the new country. Patents may be difficult to obtain since the utility of the product is public information in its original country, and therefore, not patentable. However, most countries offer "exclusivity," which is the practical equivalent of patent protection, for products that are new molecular entities. The "exclusivity" can be substantial; for example, it is 5 and 10 years in the US and EU respectively.

Two very successful examples of this strategy of obtaining approval in the US long after a product was approved in another country are metformin, a drug widely used to treat Type II diabetes, and citalopram a drug used to treat depression and related disorders. Both were submitted for US approval after long use in other countries, and both offered benefits to patients and commercial success to the companies that obtained US approval.

Collaborations Between Companies

As I hope I have made clear in the preceding sections, drug development is a complex process involving integration of many different kinds of information. There are also very strict government-reporting obligations. When drug development is split between collaborators, the complexity of the development process increases. In general, each collaborator's regulatory applications will need to include data from all the other collaborators. The complexity of doing this increases as the number of parties involved increases.

Putting a product's development into a collaboration between companies will always increase the risk of delay or failure. However, there may be business or resource limitations that require collaborative efforts. In this situation, it is very important to be sure that lines of responsibility and authority are clear, and that there are people who are empowered to make critical decisions expeditiously. Safety and efficacy information will need to be reported to regulatory bodies in a timely manner, and adverse findings by one company may have a dramatic effect on the chances of success for all the collaborators. Thus, proper procedures for sharing plans and results in an efficient and expeditious manner should be put in place before the collaboration begins. In particular, proper procedures for allowing all collaborators to meet regulatory requirements for expedited reporting of serious, unexpected adverse events must be in place before the collaboration begins.

I have seen joint development committees between two companies work well when the lines of authority and responsibility are well defined both for the individuals on the joint committee typically set up to coordinate activities and of the involved companies. One logical division of labor is between the development team doing work to support the NDA and a team from another company doing phase IV studies. Since the phase IV studies only have value if the NDA is approved, it is a good idea to let the NDA group lead the committee until the NDA is submitted. At that point, the responsibility for leading the committee can be shifted to the group responsible for phase IV.

Chapter 16 - Patents, Trademarks and Generic Names

MY INTENT IN this book has been to concentrate on the general scientific and business aspects of drug development and have largely ignored patent and trademark issues. However, they are an important part of the drug development process so I will briefly describe some important points in this Chapter.

Patents

The very high profits of the pharmaceutical industry are based, in large measure, on patent protections that limit competition, often for long periods of time after a product is approved and marketed. It is critical that the patent position of a product be as strong as possible. Projects should be reviewed by competent scientists and patent lawyers to be sure that adequate protection is available and that the product (including the active ingredients, excipients, and method of manufacture) does not infringe on patents owned by another company. This is a complex process, since there are many outstanding patents and the patents in every country where marketing is intended must be included in the patent evaluations. It is very important to be sure that patent lawyers have adequate support from key scientific staff. Often, patent issues involve subtle scientific issues that are beyond the technical expertise of any but the most specialized scientists.

Since patent coverage is so important to the commercial success of a product, it should be reviewed periodically during the development process to ensure that new information is added to the patent coverage as the development process proceeds and to ensure patent infringement has not become a problem due to the issuance of new patents.

Generic Name

Every drug substance must have a generic name. This is a name for the product which is not owned by the company sponsor and can be used by manufacturers of the generic product once the patent for a product expires. For example, Prilosec® is the trade name for a widely used proton-pump inhibitor used to treat heartburn. Its generic name is "omeprazole." Some other products in the same class are lansoprazole, pantoprazole and rabeprazole. Because these all belong to the same proton-pump inhibitor class they have similar generic names; although the trade names for these products differ widely.

In the United States, generic names are assigned by the United States Adopted Names Council (USAN). Since every NDA must include the generic name of the product, it is wise to apply to USAN early, so that they have plenty of time to assign a name. Their decision making process can take months, especially if a product is the basis for a new class and will set a precedent for the naming of future products. USAN works closely with similar naming organizations in other countries so that generic names are generally the same in all countries.

Trademarks

Every product must have a proprietary name that should have adequate trademark protection. As with patents, it is important to be sure that a proposed trademark does not infringe the trademark protection of others. Again, this is a complex process, especially when a company intends to use the same trademark in many different countries, which is a good idea if it can be done. Much of drug marketing is based on publications in scientific journals which tend to be read internationally. The use of such publications in marketing efforts is simplified if the trade name is the same in all markets of consequence. Of course, trade names must be carefully reviewed for acceptability in each country where they will be used.

Trademarks are reviewed by regulatory authorities to assure that they do not imply medical benefits beyond the approved label claims. They are also reviewed for similarity to products on the market. Similarity can lead to confusion of one product with another by dispensing pharmacists or other healthcare professionals. If a regulatory body rejects a trademark, the rejection will likely come during the NDA review process, often just before approval. Since a product cannot be approved without an approved trade name, the whole NDA approval can be delayed if the trade name is found to be unacceptable. Therefore, it is prudent to allocate plenty of time to selection of a proper trademark. All of the evaluations that will be done by the regulators during the NDA review process should be performed in advance by the company sponsor (e.g. evaluation for unacceptable implied claims, or confusion with other products).

Since the outcome of the regulatory review of the proposed trademark cannot be predicted with certainty, it is wise to have one or two "backup" trademarks that can be rapidly substituted if regulators find the initial proposal unacceptable.

It is often tempting to spend a large amount of time and money selecting a brand name. In my experience, this is not necessary for prescription drugs. The success of most prescription products is based on the scientific data supporting the marketing effort and not on the brand name. It is more reasonable to spend time and money on the brand name for a non-prescription product, where the marketing target is the over-the-counter drug consumer who is more likely to be affected by non-scientific influences, like the brand name.

National Drug Code

Every drug marketed in the United States must have a National Drug Code number, part of which is assigned by the FDA and part of which is assigned by the company marketing the product. The process of assigning this number is relatively straightforward and therefore it can be obtained during the NDA review process by submitting the proper forms to the FDA.

Product Appearance

Every drug product marketed should have a unique appearance, to allow it to be identified even after it is removed from its packaging. It would be quite time-consuming to review the appearance of every marketed drug, so the best approach to fulfilling this requirement is to imprint a trademarked company logo on the drug product, along with a code that distinguishes the particular product.

Chapter 17 - Special Considerations for Investors

Accounting Considerations

IN A CAPITALIST system, capital is supposed to be allocated to activities that generate the highest return, commonly known as "profit" or "earnings." Thus, the wisest investment is one that produces the highest profit, and thus, the method used to calculate profit is of great importance to the allocation of capital. "Generally Accepted Accounting Procedures" (GAAP) are used by the pharmaceutical industry to compute profit.

Unfortunately, while GAAP is suitable for may purposes it is not well suited for use in allocation of investment capital in the pharmaceutical business, because it distorts the true nature of a pharmaceutical company's assets. For example, if a company spends $50 million to obtain a patent worth $5 billion, using GAAP, it will show a $50 million loss until the patent is sold or monetized in some other way. Thus, by the time a company obtains approval to market a product, it has a large loss "on the books" in the form of cumulative development costs, even though the value of the product is increasing rapidly as successful development milestones are achieved. Using GAAP, returns on the capital invested are not reflected in the company's financial statements until they are sold or monetized in some other way, thus potentially understating the company's performance. This is understandable because the value of a patent or drug approval may be very difficult to assess without actually trying to sell it which is often not practical.

Conversely, GAAP will tend to overvalue a company whose drug has been successfully launched. Because GAAP doesn't take into account the fact that the inherent value of the marketed product is based upon the time-sensitive rights conferred by both its underlying patent (preventing competition), and FDA approval (granting exclusivity), GAAP fails to recognize that the product should be valued as a wasting asset. Once a product is patented and/or an NDA is approved, the clock starts ticking: the protections which help limit competition in the marketplace (thus allowing a company to recoup the costs of its development) diminish inexorably as the dates of expiration approach.

Thus, GAAP generally penalizes a company's bottom line by not recognizing the increase of value contributed by the creation of important intellectual property which will ultimately sustain the product's financial viability in the marketplace (for a limited period of time); then, compounding its error, GAAP calculates profitability from sales of a product without regard to the diminishing value of that intellectual property based on limitations on competition and exclusivity, which would typically cancel out the value of GAAP profits. These disconnects are illustrated in the following figures.

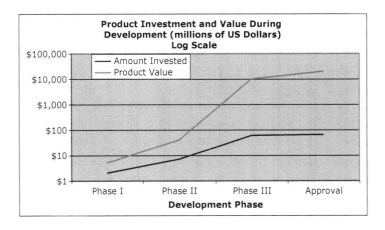

As indicated above, there is a huge increase of product value during the development process; the value of the approved product peaks at around the time of regulatory approval.

The marketing process that follows is illustrated in the next figure.

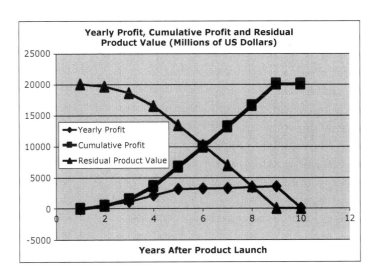

This figure illustrates that while GAAP profits from the sales of the product rapidly increase following launch, the residual value of the product is declining, as the time when the drug's patent expires and its FDA-conferred exclusivity is lost, slowly approach.

Thus, it is important to understand that the marketing of the product merely converts the value generated during its development into cash flow, part of which is then recognized as "profit" under GAAP accounting rules. However, this "profit" is somewhat illusory, because it is exactly cancelled out by the decline in the value of the product's residual patent protection. This is similar to an oil company that makes a small investment and finds a huge oil deposit; the value creation occurs with the initial discovery, even though no profit is reported at that time. As the oil is pumped from the ground, the profit earned is exactly balanced by the loss of oil reserves.

I believe, this disconnect between GAAP reporting of profits and losses is a major cause of the decline of new drug approvals. Failing to appreciate where a company's true value lies, pharmaceutical investors and even the company's financial executives tend to inadequately fund drug development relative to activities like marketing, which produce returns that are better understood and recognized.

Investors should be aware that GAAP tends to protect the pharma-industry *status quo*; it overvalues companies with products already on the market and undervalues (generally smaller) companies having R&D teams with proven abilities to obtain FDA approvals. This is a very important consideration for investors, since companies with a proven ability to get new products approved are generally undervalued in the equity markets.

Whether GAAP accounting should be modified is a complex subject far beyond the purview of this book. However, it is sufficient for industry and financial professionals to understand that GAAP profits do not accurately reflect value creation and diminution for most pharmaceutical companies. If a company was set up to discover, develop and then out-license approved products for sale by another company, its "profits" would more closely parallel its enterprise value. However, few pharma companies operate in this manner.

Annual reports and other financial statements written to communicate with investors do not contain the kind of analysis illustrated in the figures above. Companies are generally bound to report their financial results using GAAP. They tend to keep to this kind of analysis to avoid the liability that can come from analyses that are not generally accepted and therefore can be called misleading or worse by potential litigants. Nonetheless, I believe it is important to understand the amount of value creation a company can generate when contemplating a potential investment. Luckily, this is relatively easy to do since product R&D expenses, product approvals, patents and sales information are readily available for publicly traded companies.

This section is written based on the assumption that a company is marketing drugs and not biologics. The difference is important because although patent protection periods are the same for both drugs and biologics, there is not yet an established process for approval of generic biologics in the United States (there is one in the EU). Even if the patent for a biologic runs out in the US, a competitor must generally conduct many more studies to get an identical product approved in the US. Thus, biologics tend to have much less competition than non-biologic drugs.

Emotional Considerations

A company with a promising new therapy for an important illness can seem like a particularly appealing investment. Inherent, emotional responses can drive investment when the prospect of making money AND doing social good (and which has high visibility) is strong. Therefore, many investors over-value companies that promise "miracle cures" to serious or common illnesses, even when the companies have little or no ability to deliver on their promises. The corollary to this irrational investment tendency is that many investment funds make consistent profits shorting the stocks of overvalued pharmaceutical companies.

Evaluating Companies - General Considerations

Pharmaceutical companies typically release very limited information to the investment community, which makes it very difficult for investors to value products in development. For example, the acceptability of non-clinical and clinical data to regulators often hinges on esoteric details of the scientific procedures used; however, these technical details are never disclosed to the investing public.

Furthermore, because companies do not disclose what they have not done, it may be difficult to discover essential steps in the development process that have been skipped, either intentionally or unintentionally. In my experience, it is common that no one in a company has a complete understanding of the development plan's strengths and weaknesses, so it can be very difficult for management to accurately disclose them.

There are however, a few guides to evaluating development information. First, I have found that experienced, successful drug developers tend to repeat their performance again and again. Thus, if a company is using a development team that has been successful in the past, I believe it has a much higher chance of being successful in future development programs. Although it may be difficult to determine if a company still retains the development team that got their last drug approved, one potential way of doing this is to search the scientific literature and find the authors of publications of data from the products a company has already gotten approved; some of the authors listed may be from the company's development team. One can then call the company and ask for these people and see if they are still working there. Often, as discussed previously, they are gone, and if so, this would indicate that the company may have difficulty retaining critical staff.

Scientific publications of data are also helpful in another way. Data from a study of a drug in development that is published in peer-review journals has had some level of external validation by the journal peer-reviewers, and therefore, is often more reliable and complete than information from press releases or company reports.

Interactions with regulatory bodies can also be an indicator of the chance of successful drug development. A company that regularly announces that its study designs are approved in advance by major regulatory bodies is much more likely to be successful over the long run than companies that elect to proceed with important studies without prior discussions with regulators. It is very important to remember that although all clinical studies are automatically reviewed by regulators during development, the automatic regulatory review focuses primarily on protecting patient safety. The adequacy of a particular protocol for its intended purpose will generally not be evaluated by regulators until the NDA review, unless a sponsor specifically requests such a review in advance of the time the study is implemented.

Some regulatory interactions are matters of public record; for example, results of manufacturing inspections, FDA advisory committee meetings, and warning letters. While these may not be available for products in development, when available, they can provide a relatively objective assessment of the quality of a company's work product. Inspections and advisory committee meetings have been previously discussed, and Warning Letters are discussed briefly in the Glossary.

Very innovative products have an inherent appeal to investors because of the large profits that can be earned by a product that initially has limited or no competition. However, development of such products is usually considerably more risky than it would be for products that are similar to currently-marketed, widely-used medications. Because there is little or no precedent for a highly innovative product, there is more uncertainty about the kinds of toxicity it will produce and the tools that will be needed to assess them. In addition, regulatory authorities will likely request more safety data because they have fewer precedents to guide them. Thus, while very innovative products can be very profitable, they generally pose a greater risk of failure or delay. A possible exception to this would be products that have more than usual safety information, perhaps because of extensive human safety information that is based on use for another indication. Even in such a case, it should be remembered that the patient population being exposed in the new indication may be quite different, and may therefore have a different ability to tolerate the product. A clear recognition and disclosure of the additional risks associated with a very innovative product is a positive sign, suggesting a company has good insight and communication skills.

Sometimes companies with limited resources will try to take risky shortcuts in the drug development process. Two are frequently mentioned and sometimes used inappropriately. These are the Exploratory IND and the investigator-sponsored IND. These INDs are briefly defined in the Glossary, and although appropriate under limited situations, are sometimes warning signs that a company lacks the knowledge or resources to complete a standard drug development program. The same kind of concerns relate to clinical studies that a company chooses to conduct in countries with less stringent regulations than the US and Europe. While there may be very good reasons to conduct studies in countries with less stringent regulations, data from such countries is generally less compelling, because there is less validation by the government regulatory body.

For the scientifically inclined, the website, www.clinicaltrials .gov lists information about most clinical trials undertaken by pharmaceutical companies. Listing on this site was established as a way for companies to deal with criticisms about studies that were completed but whose results were never reported, in some cases because they suggested problems of some sort. Although Clinicaltrials.gov is not used to report the results of studies, it does list the times when they are completed so interested parties can ask to see the results if they are not promptly provided by the sponsoring pharmaceutical company.

In summary, the following are good portents:

1. Experienced staff with a history of successful drug approvals.
2. Publication of key data in peer-reviewed scientific journals.
3. Evidence of a close working relationship with key regulatory bodies.
4. Clear disclosure of the additional risks associated with very innovative products.

The following are warning signs:

1. Complete Response Letters requiring extensive work for approval.
2. Warning letters, consent decrees, poor establishment inspection reports or other evidence of a contentious relationship with drug regulators.
3. Use of an exploratory or investigator-sponsored IND.
4. Evidence of increased risk based on the factors summarized in Chapter 3, to the extent this kind of information is available.
5. Results of clinical studies derived from countries with less stringent regulation of clinical trials.

Specific Issues

In the following sections I will try to summarize some of the things that go wrong with development programs to assist investors who have access to reasonably detailed information about a drug in development, and who can, therefore, attempt to identify more detailed development risk factors.

Risk factors generally fall into two categories: risks of delays of the development program, and risks of delay of the ultimate approval. As mentioned in the preceding chapters, there is often a conflict between addressing these two types of risk. Since investors wish to obtain a return on their investment in the shortest possible time, there is often pressure to advance a product through the stages of development quickly, which may give the appearance that development risks have been addressed more completely than they really have. Conversely, some risks are inherent in the product itself and cannot be addressed until a significant investment of time and money have been made. In fact, some of these risks may persist even beyond the time the NDA is submitted, leading to uncertainty of the timing of marketing approval. Below are the major risks in each category and at each stage of development.

Risks and Considerations

Pre-IND

- It is common to use a very simple formulation for the initial drug product; often the active ingredient is mixed with simple excipients and placed in a gelatin capsule. Such formulations may not be suitable for commercial use, and therefore, the formulation will need to be changed as development continues. Using different formulations during development can result in difficulties justifying use of data obtained with an early formulation to support approval of the final formulation. It is important to be sure the development team is aware of this issue and has an effective plan to deal with it.

- It is important that the drug substance and product have adequate stability to make a practical product. A shelf-life of at least two years is usually required for a product to be commercially viable. Seek information about stability from the company.

- It is important to be sure that the drug substance does not degrade into toxic substances during storage. Seek information about the toxicology of degradants from the company.

- Mutagenicity - Seek information from the company and evaluate published data on mutagenicity of chemically-related compounds. Mutagenicity often predicts carcinogenicity, and for all but the most critical life-saving therapies, carcinogenicity is usually a complete obstacle to marketing approval.

- Severe Toxicity - Toxicity which occurs suddenly as the dose is raised, occurs near clinically-useful doses, or that will be difficult to evaluate in people (e.g. microscopic tissue changes in organs that are not easily accessible for biopsy) is particularly troubling. The safety issues identified in animal studies have a strong influence on the safety evaluations required in the clinical program. Rare or very severe toxicity will likely increase the size and/or duration of safety evaluations in clinical trials, sometimes dramatically. Seek data from the company or published data regarding toxicity in non-clinical studies.

- Unfavorable pharmacokinetics - Low absorption of drugs (less than about 50%) is usually associated with blood levels that vary considerably from day-to-day and patient-to-patient. This may present a significant problem if blood levels associated with toxicity are close to those required for efficacy. In general, the blood half-life of the active substance should be at least as half the proposed dosing interval. For drugs where only a limited duration of action is desired (sleep aids, diagnostic aids) the half-life may be a very important predictor of clinical utility. Half-lives that are too short can often be addressed by modifying the drug product so that the active ingredient is released more slowly. Skipping this step may create the appearance of progress at the expense of the ultimate success of the development effort. Seek information from the company or from scientific literature about the extent of absorption, half-life of blood levels, and dose intervals. Animals typically eliminate drugs more quickly than humans, but extrapolations from animal data can be used to predict an approximate human half-life.

- Metabolites - Each metabolite has the potential for both efficacy and toxicity. Metabolites that do not contribute to efficacy have only potential for toxicity. Therefore, products with multiple, non-efficacious, metabolites have a proportionately higher risk of toxicity. Seek information from both the company and scientific literature regarding the existence, efficacy and route of elimination of the active drug and any metabolites.

- Toxicity that mimics the disorder being treated - An example of this kind of toxicity would be an antibiotic that causes fever as a side-effect. Since fever can be a sign of the infection the antibiotic is used to treat, physicians using it will be unsure if a fever is due to the disease or the antibiotic, greatly complicating use of the product. This can also complicate the drug development process. Seek information from the company or scientific literature about toxicity that could mimic the disorder being treated.

- Effects on cardiac conduction – There are standard evaluations of this at the pre-clinical stage. Since adverse effects on cardiac conduction can be a significant obstacle to marketing approval, they should be evaluated before advancing a compound into human studies.

Phase I

- Many of the same issues listed above for the initial animal studies apply to the results of initial human studies as well. It is especially important to assure an adequate safety profile, metabolism, and pharmacokinetics. The results of phase I studies are often presented at scientific meetings or published in scientific journals and if available, they can often be obtained via literature searches and/or requests for information from the company or authors. An especially important concern is a comparison of a drug's half-life in blood with its proposed dosing interval. If there is a mismatch, the company should have a good explanation for how it will be addressed.

- Effects on cardiac conduction – These are addressed to some degree by initial phase I studies. If the results are not included in the publicly available data, reassurance from the company should be obtained. The results of the standard evaluation of effects on cardiac conduction in healthy human volunteers should also be obtained by the company. If this data evaluation is not obtained early in the clinical development process, the deficit should be considered an additional risk for ultimate marketing approval.

Phase II

The primary objective of phase II is to obtain evidence of efficacy and to determine the doses required to achieve it. Beginning phase III without definitive results from phase II should generally be considered a sign of high risk for a new chemical entity that is not known to be effective based on other data. Specific issues are listed below:

- In general, the phase II study should be done using a double-blind design within which neither the company nor the investigator(s) doing the study are aware of who is receiving the investigational product and who is receiving the well-characterized control treatment. It is critically important that the study treatments are not disclosed until all the data are obtained and the database is locked. The statistical methods to be used for analysis should also be fixed prior to the time the treatments are unblinded. This information can often be obtained from results presented at scientific meetings or published in scientific journals. Such presentations and publications are a good sign that the company is allowing some level of peer review of their data. In many cases, a well-designed phase II study can be used as a pivotal study to support the efficacy of the product in the NDA. It is often a good idea to ask the company if the phase II data can be used for this purpose because it eliminates the need for one of the usually two required phase III studies. If the company states that the phase II results are acceptable as a pivotal proof of efficacy, ask if this has been verified by a major governmental regulatory authority. If so, this is a very promising sign.

- During the time when phase II is being conducted, consideration of evaluations of effects of food and other drugs on the absorption and elimination of the investigational product should be either underway or in late planning stages. Since companies rarely publish their development plans in detail, the status and results of these evaluations must be requested directly from company representatives. Food effects and drug interactions can have a dramatic influence on difficulty of conducting phase III studies and also on the potential market for a drug, and therefore should be considered seriously.

Phase III

- Companies often disclose the design and other details of their phase III studies in press releases or company presentations. This can allow a check of their power calculations as well as their projected time and costs. It is important that the company state that the design of phase III has been approved in advance by the FDA and other regulatory bodies.
- During or prior to phase III, manufacturing scale-up will need to be completed to assure adequate supplies of drug product for the phase III studies as well as adequate stability data on large batches that need to be included in the NDA. This adequacy of kind of information should be discussed with the company.
- Also during phase III, final toxicology work must be completed. This often includes obtaining results of carcinogenicity studies. Since a positive carcinogenicity study can be a block to marketing approval, this risk factor should always be kept in mind, especially if

mutagenicity studies suggest this is a significant risk. The company should be asked to confirm that the FDA has officially approved the design and doses being used in the carcinogenicity studies, and that the studies are being implemented without ANY changes to the protocol approved by the FDA.

- Phase III studies sometimes mandate that interim safety analyses be conducted before the study is completed; usually by an independent "Data Monitoring Committee." While this can be a routine matter, a requirement for this kind of interim analyses by regulators suggests that they are especially concerned about the potential for serious toxicity consistent with an increased level of risk for delay and/or ultimate marketing approval.

Chapter 18 - Case Studies and Personal Anecdotes

I AM NOT A historian. The cases I recount in this section represent my personal recollection of events. I have not conducted an extensive review of available documents to confirm my recollections. Nonetheless, I consider the following to be illustrative of the challenges of drug development, and therefore, I think you will find them instructive if not completely accurate historically.

Tacrine

Tacrine had been licensed as a drug outside the US (I believe is was approved as a muscle relaxant) for many years at the time sporadic reports of its activity as a treatment for Alzheimer's disease gained attention in the US. These reports motivated the Warner Lambert Company to consider developing tacrine as a treatment for Alzheimer's disease. At the time Warner started the development of tacrine, there were no other FDA-approved treatments for Alzheimer's disease, and therefore no precedent for getting a product approved. Thus, Warner decided to work closely with FDA. Based on publicly available information, mostly from information I gleaned at FDA advisory committee meetings, Warner held many meetings with FDA to discuss their planned development program. It seems that many outside academic consultants were also involved in designing the program. Because there was some anecdotal information that seemed to suggest that the response to tacrine varied considerably from person to person, a very complex phase III study was undertaken that involved titrating each patient to his or her own maximally effective dose. In my experience, such a design for a pivotal efficacy study was unprecedented and it should have been clear to anyone with statistical knowledge that the interpretation of the results of such a study would be complex and open to challenge. This would be especially true if the therapeutic effects were small. Based on the early studies of tacrine, it was clear that the beneficial effects, if present, were likely to be very small implying a significant risk that the results of the study would be challenged. Thus, the study design agreed to by FDA and Warner Lambert was clearly risky and as should have been expected, the study failed to show compelling efficacy.

Furthermore, it was clear from the chemical structure of tacrine that it had a high risk of toxic effects unrelated to its desired mechanism of action. Thus, it was not surprising when the results of the pivotal study showed a high risk of liver toxicity.

How is it possible that a large company like Warner Lambert could initiate a study with both a high chance of failing to show efficacy and also a high risk of showing undesired toxicity? Based my observations at the FDA advisory committee meetings for tacrine, I would surmise the following explanation.

At the time tacrine development was initiated, there was a large demand for treatments of Alzheimer's disease and it probably seemed reasonable to try extraordinary measures to get a drug approved. My guess is that Warner tried to design a study they thought would maximize the chance of showing a statistically significant benefit relative to placebo. The company probably reasoned that the FDA would not be overly critical of the study design because of the large public demand for an approved treatment for Alzheimer's disease. Thus, Warner was willing (if only in its corporate subconscious) to take the chance of doing a study that would be open to question from the scientific point of view, in return for increasing what they thought was their chance of getting a numerically acceptable result. In addition, the complex study design was probably supported by academics who had proposed that the response to tacrine was variable among patients. This academic support for the complex study design probably further supported Warner's decision to pursue it.

FDA likely perceived the situation in a very different way. Although the FDA apparently agreed to Warner's study design, it was undoubtedly aware of the potential to get statistically-significant benefit for the drug relative to placebo based purely or partially on "adjustment" of the analysis once the final data were in hand. Thus, the FDA, as required by law, probably felt that it had little leeway in allowing any kind of adjustments to the data analysis agreed to with Warner prior to completion of the study. Also, taking a more global view, FDA probably reasoned that any exception granted to Warner would probably set a precedent that other companies with similar products could cite possibly leading to a flood of weak NDA applications that FDA would have a hard time controlling.

Ultimately, the data for Warner's first study did not show statistically significant benefit for tactrine versus placebo when analyzed as Warner had agreed with FDA. While Warner was able to get statistically significant results by adjusting the analysis, as would be expected the FDA would only accept the analysis agreed to before the study was unblinded.

As I recall, at the FDA advisory committee meeting where the results of the study were discussed, Warner claimed that the FDA had verbally agreed to change the method of analysis of the study from the written protocol previously approved by the FDA. In other words, that the signed agreement with FDA had been modified by a verbal communication. As I recall, a representative from Warner went so far as to suggest the FDA Division Director had been untruthful for denying that such a verbal agreement had been made. In response, the FDA Division Director calmly projected a copy of the written protocol, signed by Warner's representatives specifying the analysis that FDA wanted. This highlights the need to be sure that agreements with FDA be are committed to writing.

The FDA advisory committee voted to reject approval of tacrine and FDA followed the committee's vote.

What lessons can one draw from this? First of all, innovative study designs should be approached with great caution. It is often hard to get FDA to agree to a design it has not accepted before and when it does FDA tends to be skeptical of the results. Also, the failure of the study to show definitive efficacy was at least in part due to the difficultly of predicting the results due to its unusual design which had little or no precedent. Ultimately, tacrine and other Alzheimer's drugs were approved based on more conventional study designs.

A second lesson is clear. Always, always, always, get agreements with FDA in writing, and make sure that the written agreement is being interpreted in the same way by your company and FDA. Beware of the temptation to think you can force FDA to accept your interpretation of an ambiguous situation. FDA is required by law to interpret data conservatively, and in almost all cases, this is what they will do. Thus, clear written agreements, confirmed in writing on multiple occasions with the relevant division director are critical to successful relations with FDA especially when "innovative" development programs are undertaken. Simply put, don't take unnecessary chances.

Gancyclovir

My understanding of the gancyclovir development program is based on my attendance at an FDA advisory meeting called to review the NDA, where the FDA and the sponsor, Syntex Corporation, told very different stories about how the development program was supposed to have been done. I have no way of know which story, if either, was true. However, I believe the situation, as I recall it, is instructive since it illustrates common issues that are important even if they did not occur exactly as I recall them in this particular case.

Gancyclovir was developed for treatment of cytomegalovirus retinitis. This tragic illness occurs commonly among HIV-infected individuals and without treatment leads inexorably to blindness in all afflicted patients. As I recall, at the time of the FDA advisory meeting, it was agreed that no case of spontaneously improved vision had been observed in any patient with CMV retinitis. According to my recollection, Syntex asserted that the

FDA had agreed that no placebo group was required to show efficacy of their product because any improvement of vision in a patient with CMV retinitis would be acceptable evidence that the drug was efficacious. At the time the gancyclovir studies were initiated, there was no known effective treatment for CMV retinitis, so a placebo-controlled study would have been possible. However, Syntex elected to do the uncontrolled study they believed the FDA had agreed to.

At the advisory committee meeting, FDA denied that it had agreed to an uncontrolled study as the basis for approval of gancyclovir, and their representative gave a general discussion of the scientific justification for requiring placebo-controlled studies as part of his review of Syntex's NDA. He also mentioned that the Food Drug and Cosmetic Act, as amended, requires adequate and well-<u>controlled</u> studies as the basis for approval. Based on the FDA's presentation, the advisory committee voted to recommend that Syntex's application be rejected, and the FDA followed this advice and did not approve the product.

Now, the story really gets interesting. The infectious disease community's opinion differed from that of the Advisory Committee and the FDA. By and large, they accepted Syntex's data as showing that gancyclovir was effective at preventing blindness. Thus, when Syntex attempted to initiate placebo-controlled studies of gancyclovir in order to comply with the FDA's mandate, they could not do so, because to provide placebos to a portion of the patient population who could go blind without the active ingredient was felt to be unethical by the infectious disease doctors who were needed to implement the placebo-controlled studies. In addition, because essentially everyone but FDA believed gancyclovir was needed to prevent blindness in afflicted AIDS patients, Syntex was compelled to supply it to patients who requested it. Since gancyclovier was not approved for sale, Syntex had to supply it under a "compassionate use" program, and I assume, absorb the large costs giving the drug away for free and collecting uncontrolled data from the compassionate-use patients and watching its patent life dwindle while competitors moved their products through development. I believe that ultimately, FDA did approve gancyclovir without placebo-controlled data. However, this was several years after the initial rejection.

It is difficult to know why Syntex did not do a placebo-controlled study at the beginning of their development program, while it was still possible to do so. Perhaps, it wanted to maximize the chances of benefiting patients by not randomizing any of them to placebo. Perhaps, it felt that an uncontrolled design was more likely to be successful. It does appear, however, that by using an uncontrolled study design, Syntex delayed its approval by several years, probably losing large amounts of revenue and limiting the availability of an important drug for patients who needed it desperately. (the large paperwork burden of a compassionate use program tends to limit the availability of products to rather sophisticated physicians and patients). The lesson once again is to avoid unusual study designs, if possible, and to be sure that any agreement with FDA is confirmed in writing on multiple occasions.

A Disgusting Adverse Event

One of the products I was involved in developing was out-licensed to a major, multinational pharmaceutical company that took over reporting adverse events to the FDA. As discussed earlier, if such adverse events suggest a new significant risk to the patients in clinical trials, they must be reported promptly to FDA. As part of the licensing agreement, I received copies of the reports submitted to the FDA. One such report recorded a patient who developed prolonged diarrhea. He was eventually admitted to the hospital because the diarrhea did not resolve at home, i.e. because he did not recover from his diarrhea.

Because this adverse event occurred in a study outside the United States and was not recorded in English the intial report form had to be translated before it could be submitted to FDA. The translation stated that the patient was admitted to the hospital "because the diarrhea could not be recovered." The image of trying to "recover" diarrhea provoked some pretty disgusting images, and gave the people in my group a good laugh.

I can't imagine what the people at FDA thought when they saw such carelessness. Obviously, submitting reports with this kind of careless error to FDA creates the impression that the company is not paying careful attention to the safety of the patients in its clinical trials. This can result in all kinds of extra burdens on the company, depending on the FDA's level of concern.

It is noteworthy that the translated adverse event report had a signoff page that contained 23 approval signatures. Apparently, none of the 23 people who signed off on the report read it carefully or perhaps at all. My guess is that each of the people who signed thought that the other signors had or would read the report before it was submitted to FDA, but in the end, none of them did.

I think this example shows how dispersing responsibility among too many people is damaging to the quality of end product.

CGIC

The CGIC (Clinical Global Impression of Change) was one of the assessments chosen to evaluate the efficacy of drugs in Alzheimer's disease (AD) patients. Its history provides an interesting insight into the drug regulatory process. During the early development of tacrine, the first product approved for AD treatment, it became clear that its therapeutic benefit was relatively small and that it was not a cure for Alzheimer's disease. However, it was also relatively clear that tacrine did provide some benefit, when assessed using the Alzheimer's disease assessment scale, cognitive subscale ("ADAS-cog", for short) a scale that was well accepted as very sensitive and accurate. It was also clear that, tacrine caused liver toxicity and its structure suggested that it might well be carcinogenic (this was later proved through comprehensive carcinogenicity studies). The FDA was in a quandary; the balance between safety and efficacy was unclear. How much clinical benefit was required to balance the possible risks? What about the fact that there was no treatment available for Alzheimer's patients and that the patients generally had a limited life expectancy and therefore were unlikely to get cancer from tacrine? Wasn't any drug better than nothing? Much discussion was held on this safety/efficacy balance in public forums, and I am sure much more was held in private within the FDA.

Eventually, the discussion devolved into an attempt to define what was a meaningful improvement in the symptoms of Alzheimer's disease. Naturally, there were many opinions on this. Some held that any measurable improvement was enough to justify approval, with appropriate warnings about safety. Others felt it would be wasteful to approve a product with very minor benefits that would drain money away from other parts of the healthcare system.

It was the unenviable task of the FDA to determine what would be considered a meaningful clinical benefit. Since this would likely be a subjective judgment, it seemed obvious that whatever decision was made would be criticized. The FDA was reluctant to rely on the ADAS-cog alone because it was a very sensitive test and could detect improvements that were too small to be noticed by patients and physicians in a typical healthcare setting. The FDA came up with the following ingenious solution. They decided to require that efficacy be demonstrated using two separate tests. One could be the very sensitive ADAS-cog. However, the other had to be a test of "global function" of the patient. In particular, the so-called clinical global impression of change (CGIC) could not involve any pre-specified performance testing of the patient and the CGIC rater was required to be blinded to the results of all the other kinds of clinical testing of the patient. The results had to be reported using a 7-point scale, ranging from much better to much worse scores. The criteria for this evaluation were vague, since, for example, one person's mildly improved could be another person's much better. In addition, by requiring the results to be recorded using a 7-point scale (rather than allowing a continuous scale which could take on values like "2.65") the statistical power was reduced.

From the scientific point of view, the CGIC was a very poor tool for evaluating clinical efficacy. However, the FDA saw this as a strength, since this poor tool could only detect large clinical effects. Modest clinical effects would not produce statistically significant differences between an active treatment and placebo in a study of a reasonable number of patients. The

FDA reasoned that if a statistically significant improvement in CGIC could be demonstrated, it would automatically have to be clinically meaningful because the CGIC was such an insensitive tool. Thus, the usual scientific objective of trying to use very precise and sensitive tools to assess effects was inverted, and very poor tool was preferred. Relying on statistical significance using a poor tool removed much of the clinical judgment from the approval process and this protected the FDA reviewers from criticism for what would have otherwise been very subjective decisions about the clinical importance of small changes of ADAS-cog. In the years since the original FDA guidance on approval of drugs for the treatment of Alzheimer's disease, the requirements for approval have slowly changed. There are now a wider spectrum of assessments accepted by regulators. However, in the early days things were very different.

Arithmetic

One would think that a company preparing to develop a new medicine that would be used by millions of people would be sure it could handle simple arithmetic. However, I have reproduced a table that I found in the course of reviewing a draft FDA application.

Animal	Change from Pretreatment
1	0
2	0
3	0
Average Change from Pretreatment	27

The table shows the results of an animal experiment. Each animal had no change (i.e. change is listed as 0). The average change is listed as "27", a very obvious mistake. Since I had found numerous mistakes in the reports of the company, and it was very time consuming to review and correct each report in detail, I went to the head of research and development to discuss what could be done. He looked at the table thought for a few minutes and told me that while he understood the problem, there was nothing he could do. Of course I was absolutely flabbergasted that this kind of sloppiness could be tolerated in a major corporation. Unfortunately, I have found this kind of problem to be much more common than I would have expected. The only solution is to make sure that management has a sincere commitment to quality and accuracy, which is communicated throughout the company both by instruction and example. Investors should be on the lookout for small inconsistencies in presentations. They often indicate a careless approach to accuracy that is usually incompatible with successful drug development.

The Projected Market for Alzheimer's Disease Treatments

When I first discussed developing a new treatment for Alzheimer's disease with people in the pharmaceutical industry, the reaction of most was to tell me that such a product was impractical because the market was too small. This made no sense to me, because as a physician, I was aware of the large unmet medical need for dementia therapies. When I probed the issue, I found that the conclusion that the market for Alzheimer's disease therapies was small was based on market research that showed very small dollar volume for such products. However, what the market researchers failed to understand, was that the sales of Alzheimer's products were small because there were no approved products on the market. It seemed logical to me that once a product was approved for treatment of Alzheimer's, the market would be created, and this is exactly what happened. However, at the time, the idea that the market was small was remarkably common and widely accepted. I have since seen this same kind of problem in many other situations where market research must be adjusted for the likely impact of novel therapies in order to be accurate.

Proton Pump Inhibitors

Proton pump inhibitors inhibit acid production by the stomach. At the time proton pump inhibitors were discovered, the main treatments for peptic ulcers and heartburn (gastro-esophageal reflux) were antacids and histamine$_2$ receptor blockers. The proton-pump inhibitors were much more effective at reducing acid levels in the stomach and esophagus than existing treatments but with the exception, (to my knowledge) of two companies, Astra and Merck, no one thought that this was important. The almost-universal belief was that existing treatments were adequate.

Astra's proton-pump inhibitor caused very unusual stomach tumors in rats. This was thought by many to be a complete impediment to regulatory approval, as is often the case when animal tumors are caused a new drug. However, in this case there were extenuating circumstances. For example, the tumors found in rats did not seem to cause any disability. In fact, the rats with tumors seemed to live longer than rats in the untreated placebo group. Furthermore, the types of tumors seen in the rats almost never caused any problem in people and were typically seen as incidental findings when an autopsy was done for other reasons.

At the time, I recognized that the tumors would be a significant obstacle for regulatory approval. However, because the tumors did not appear to cause disease, it seemed reasonable that this could be overcome, in due course, by a diligent and talented development team. In addition, the peptic-ulcer, heartburn market was the largest therapeutic market in the pharmaceutical industry at the time and it seemed logical that having one of the most effective products in that market should be very profitable.

Finally, inhibition of stomach-acid secretion was known to be highly correlated with clinical efficacy in the treatment of ulcers and heartburn, so the results of relatively easy to conduct acid secretion studies were likely to be highly predictive of the results of much larger, higher-risk clinical efficacy studies. For all these reasons, I believed that a new proton-pump inhibitor was likely to be a great commercial success. Best of all, Merck, one of the top drug development companies of the day, was also pushing ahead and dealing with all the complexities of getting a new class of drug approved, making the path for the second product much clearer. Thus, a second-to-market proton-pump inhibitor, like the one I proposed for development, seemed to fulfill all the criteria for successful development and commercial success. However, aside from the people at Astra and Merck, few people shared my assessment, until Merck got its product, Prilosec®, approved, and it was an enormous success. Then, every major pharmaceutical company in the world wanted a proton-pump inhibitor, and the proton-pump inhibitor drugs became the most successful drug class in the industry for many years leading to many, many billions of dollars in profit for my project.

I think this example supports the criteria for selection of new products outlined in this book. When these objective criteria can be successfully applied, they lead to almost unimaginable success, both from the commercial point of view of from the point of view of benefit to patients. However, while the criteria are relatively simple, as discussed previously, applying them can be very challenging.

Criminal Misbranding

As I described in the beginning of this book, a drug consists of the actual drug product, plus its approved labeling. In this context, the "approved labeling" includes the Package Insert approved by the relevant regulatory authority, for example, the FDA.

All promotional material that is used by a company (print advertisements, handouts given out by sales representatives, TV advertising, etc.) must be based on the efficacy and safety data included in the Package Insert. If a product is promoted using claims outside those included in the Package Insert, or if critical safety data from the Package Insert is not included in promotional material, then from the regulators' point of view, the "product" (including the labeling) being promoted is different from the "product" that was approved. Such a product is designated as "misbranded."

Penalties for marketing a misbranded product can vary from an FDA request to stop, to more serious civil and criminal liability. An example is the case of Purdue Frederick.

According to the New York Times (May 10, 2007), Purdue pled guilty to promoting its controlled-release OxyContin® as a product that "posed a lower threat of abuse and addiction to patients" than immediate-release products. This would be misbranding, if there was no such superiority claim in the Oxycontin Package Insert. In addition, most controlled-release products can be easily converted to immediate release if they are broken or chewed, and this is usually mentioned as a Package Insert warning. Of course, for a drug-abuser, a Package Insert caution about chewing or breaking the tablets may not be a warning but rather an instruction manual for abuse.

News reports are replete with the problems associated with OxyContin abuse, and this high visibility made severe government sanctions a high probability. As outlined in the Times article, Purdue and three top executives from an affiliated company pled guilty to criminal charges. The company's total of criminal and civil penalties was reported as $600 million. The executives agreed to pay a total of $34.5 million dollars in fines, even though the prosecution was not required to show knowledge or intent on the executives' part.

Death Penalty

This story may be entirely apocryphal although I heard it from a source who has always been reliable.

There have been a number of scandals involving regulation of the pharmaceutical industry. One of the largest occurred following changes to the Food and Drug Law that allowed the generic drug business to come into existence. As can be imagined, when the law was amended to allow 505j approvals, a number of new companies were started, and some of them obtained generic drug approvals using fraudulent data or influenced the generic drug approval process through bribes to FDA officials. Ultimately, the frauds were discovered and a number of people were prosecuted and some were jailed. This natural reaction to illegal behavior was followed by a period when FDA personnel were subject to intense scrutiny. I will relate a story I heard about one of them. Whether true or not, many FDA personnel behave as though it could happen.

This is a story about an FDA reviewer who was subjected to routine inquiries about taking bribes from industry representatives. He denied receiving any improper payments or gifts. Ultimately, one or more pharmaceutical companies reported that their employees had, on a number of occasions taken the FDAer out to dinner and paid the full check. The FDA reviewer then admitted that he had gotten the free dinners but he maintained that he hadn't mentioned them because he considered the value of a few dinners to be so minimal that they didn't represent a meaningful gift. The Justice Department did not agree. They successfully prosecuted the FDA reviewer and he was sentenced to several years in jail.

This particular FDA reviewer happened to be diabetic. During his incarceration, he was not able to have the special shoes he needed to avoid the foot infections that can be a terrible problem for diabetics. By the time he was released from prison, he had severe foot problems, which ultimately worsened. Eventually he died from them. Thus, in this possibly true story, the FDA reviewer essentially got the death penalty for accepting a few free dinners.

I don't know if this story is really true. However, a good drug development person should behave as if such things could happen. While it is fine to try to maintain a congenial relationship with FDA personnel, never, ever offer anything of value to them, not a cup of coffee or a shared cab ride (unless they pay their share).

Heart Attack

As the reader may gather, drug development is not for the faint-hearted. There are many balls to juggle simultaneously and little room for error. Sometimes the stress can be enough to make a project leader look and feel like he/she may actually have a heart attack and die.

I had been working on a major project for a number of years. The phase II data looked interesting, but was not conclusive. There was no money to repeat it, and so it was decided to take the risk of implementing phase III based on our best guess of the appropriate doses. Two phase III studies were required for regulatory approval, and although it would have been desirable to do more than two (in case one didn't work), there was only money to support two.

After a number of years of preliminary work and implementation of the two phase III studies, we met with the project statisticians to be sure the final phase III study databases were complete and checked, and then to authorize un-blinding of the treatment codes of the two studies so that the data from the drug and control groups could be compared. The computer programs to do the analysis were all written. To be sure that the programs worked properly, the statisticians had tested the programs by making up treatment assignments for each patient without regard to what the patients had actually received, and verifying that the programs worked properly with these "dummy" treatment codes.

We reviewed the integrity of the database containing the blinded results of the studies and to the best of our ability, assured that all was in order, and then signed the papers authorizing the treatment codes to be unblinded, affirming that the treatment codes, were still properly sealed and authorizing the statisticians to unseal the computer files containing the real treatment assignments and to analyze the results of the two studies.

The statisticians told us it would take about half an hour to do the analysis of each study and that they would be done sequentially. We waited in a conference room. The air was electric. Tens of millions of dollars of investment hung in the balance. The treatment options of millions of patients would or would not be expanded. Perhaps, billions of dollars of revenue and the future reputation of the development team would be made or lost based on the results of the statistical analyses. The company CEO and Board of Directors were waiting by the phone a number of time zones away.

The minutes ticked by. About 20 minutes after we authorized the code break, the door opened and the statisticians walked in. I knew immediately by the looks on their faces that the news was good. Sure enough, the primary study endpoints had achieved a very high level of statistical improvement relative to the control treatment. In addition, the safety profile looked good. One down, one to go (since both studies had to be successful to support marketing approval).

The statisticians left the room to analyze the second study. Time ticked by even more slowly. The second study could still theoretically fail just by chance, so nothing was guaranteed. Twenty minutes had passed, and there were no statisticians! Thirty minutes, no one. Finally, after 45 minutes, the door swung open, and the statisticians walked in. I could tell by the looks on their faces that there was a problem. They started presenting the results of the second study, trying to put a good face on a devastatingly bad outcome. The drug looked a little better than control here but worse there... I couldn't believe it. How could one study have worked so well and the other be a complete disaster? The people in the room later told me I looked so horrified that they thought I would just have a heart attack and die on the spot.

The positive results of the first study were very strong, making it exceedingly unlikely that they occurred because of a mistake, and there was no scientific reason why the two studies should have given such disparate results. After about a minute, I decided it was not possible for the studies to be so inconsistent, and that the statisticians must have made a mistake with the analysis of the second study. They insisted that they had checked and rechecked their analysis, which was why the second analysis had taken so long. I told them I still didn't believe it and they should check again; that I was absolutely sure they had made a mistake analyzing the results of the second study. Ultimately they said they would check again, but I knew by their tone of voice that they viewed me with pity, a clinical development person who just couldn't accept the reality of his failure.

The CEO and Board waited in their other time zone. We waited in the conference room. An eternity later, the statisticians re-entered the room with hangdog looks on their faces. They had used the "dummy" treatment randomization for the analysis of the second study. The one they used had been made up to test the analysis programs, and had nothing to do with the actual treatments the patients had received during the study. When the statisticians used the correct treatment codes, the results showed a highly significant improvement in the active-treated patients relative to the control-treated patients. I wish I could say I was happy, but really all I could feel was relief that I didn't accept the initial results presented to us at face value. The CEO was happy, the Board of Directors was happy and I was relieved I didn't drop dead from a heart attack. If I had, would anyone have ever noticed the error? Would the company have had to report my death to the FDA as a drug-related?

Ultimately, our faith in the second analysis was vindicated by regulatory agencies that repeated the analysis and got the same answer; highly statistically significant improvement by our drug in both studies.

This incident is only one of many similar ones I could write about and is an example of an important principle. A good drug development person should always apply a healthy dose of common sense to the drug development process. When things don't make sense, push hard to resolve the inconsistencies. If I had accepted the initial results presented to me, it is possible that the approval of my company's drug could have been delayed for years denying patients an important therapy and my company billions of dollars of revenue.

Chapter 19 - Safety Monitoring

STUFF HAPPENS, IN life and in clinical development. So, it is inevitable that participants in clinical trials will suffer adverse events. The key is to separate random adverse events from those that result from drug therapy. There are several strategies that can be used to monitor for drug-related adverse events during development. It is important to use these strategies in an objective manner, always erring on the side of protecting the participants in the clinical trials and the patients who will take the product after it is marketed. Although it may be tempting to ignore subtle evidence of potential safety problems, it is far easier to deal with them early, than to wait until they affect a large number of people when their economic and legal consequences may be much more severe.

In the initial evaluation of a new molecular entity, one is frequently confronted with toxicity in the animal studies that will be very difficult to monitor in humans. This is because animal studies allow evaluations that would be unethical to do in humans. For example, animals are often killed and autopsied at the end of a study. It is important to consider the impact of such of such difficult-to-monitor adverse events on the subsequent development and marketing of the proposed product. If the safety of the product cannot be adequately assessed in humans, it may never be possible to assemble a safety database adequate to support the approval and/or successful marketing of the product.

Phase I study results often give hints of safety issues that will appear in later studies. It is important to follow up on any trend noted in the phase I studies.

An important strategy for assessing safety is to carefully consider the likely adverse consequences of a product's desired clinical effects, and plan to monitor for them during the development process. For example, a drug designed to lower blood pressure could lower it too much in some patients, so it would be logical to monitor this carefully during development. In addition, since fainting, falling, dizziness, etc., can be a consequence of low blood pressure, these should be looked for as well as evidence of organ problems related to lowering of blood flow. In this particular example, some of the adverse events are relatively common, (e.g. dizziness) and can be expected to occur from time to time in healthy untreated people. Thus, they can be most easily detected if there is an untreated placebo-control group available for comparison. Use of such a control group is almost always a very good idea. However in some cases, it is unethical to use a placebo control group, for example when the illness being treated is serious and other approved treatments are available. In such cases, another active drug can be generally be used for comparison. The collection of safety information based on expected adverse events should be "built in" to the development program from the beginning and data monitored carefully at frequent intervals.

A similar approach should be used to look for the adverse events noted in the animal safety studies. Evaluations for these adverse events should be included in the clinical studies and carefully monitored as clinical development proceeds.

International guidelines for reporting of adverse events require that any newly-identified risk of treatment must be reported to relevant regulatory authorities within specified timeframes. These reporting requirements should be codified in standard operating procedures and also serve as a good way of monitoring safety internally.

It is sometimes possible to address difficult safety concerns by restricting the kinds of patients who will use a product. Thus, if a product is suspected to have the potential to cause birth defects when given to pregnant women, it should not be given to them, even though the toxic effect has not been definitively proven. If a product is suspected to multiply the risk of heart attacks, it may still be usable, if its use is restricted to patients who have a very low risk of heart attacks prior to treatment.

Recently, large clinical trials have been initiated to evaluate the frequency of rare, severe and/or fatal adverse events of new drugs. In such studies, the new product is often compared with an older product that is believed to be very safe. From the pharmaceutical company's point of view, the objective of the study is to show that their new product is not more dangerous than the older established product, in spite of prior evidence of an increased risk. In a number of cases, however, the safety problem hinted at in earlier studies has been established as real in more definitive studies, with the new product showing an increased risk for severe adverse events and/or death.

I believe there are serious ethical issues raised by a study where there is a significant possibility that the test product will be shown to have this kind of problem. If there is a significant risk to the study participants, it may be much better to simply restrict the use of the product to patients where the safety is well accepted, rather than testing the product in higher risk patients and finding that it causes severe or fatal outcomes.

I have been involved in the pharmaceutical industry long enough to have seen the cycle of concern about drug safety. The last cycle began a few decades ago when there were many complaints that the drug approval process was too slow. The Food and Drug Law was amended to provide mandatory review times that the FDA had to meet. There was additional political pressure to allow new drugs to be approved in marginal situations, where they previously might have been rejected.

Over the last decade or so, we have seen an upswing in the number of products that had significant safety issues identified after they were approved for marketing. In some cases, the products were actually removed from the market. This upswing in post-approval problems is a natural consequence of the changes in the Food and Drug Law enacted years ago. Speeding up the approval process leaves less time to carefully evaluate clinical data, thereby increasing the risk of mistakes. This is not necessarily bad. There will always be a trade-off between speed and quality, and it is a societal and political judgment call as to where the line should be drawn. Unfortunately, decisions about drug safety are often seen in a purely binary context: that is, the product should or should not be on the market. I believe that in a significant number of cases the real situation is more nuanced and safety issues could be addressed by changing the way a product is used; for example by restricting the population to those patients believed to be at the lowest risk of toxicity.

Chapter 20 - Who Gets Drugs Approved

IN 2007, A total of 19 new chemical entities and new biologics were approved; the lowest number since 1983, according to an article on bloomberg.com. Of these, two were not really "new drugs" in sense of being novel therapeutics; one was a diagnostic agent (Ammonia N-13, a radio-isotope), and one was a pro-drug for amfetamine, a drug that has been available for many years.

According to Pharma, the trade association for large brand pharmaceutical companies, a total of $55.3 billion dollars was spent on drug development during 2006. Of course, some of the R&D expense reported by Pharma was expended on products that would not be considered new chemical entities; for example products approved as 505b2 applications, vaccines, diagnostics, etc. However, it is likely that the bulk of the R&D expense was devoted to the development of NCEs. Assuming all the R&D expense was for NCEs, and simply dividing the total expense by the number of NCE approvals, the result is an average cost of $2.91 billion per NCE approval. Assuming a gross profit of around 50% of sales, this means that each product must sell $5.82 billion before its cost of development can be recouped. Few products can attain this level of sales in a reasonable period of time, and therefore, the high R&D expenditure is clearly not sustainable.

It is heartening, however, that there are still some companies capable of getting NCEs approved, and it is worth recognizing that two companies obtained two NCE approvals in 2007, this most difficult of years.

The following table shows all the NCEs approved in 2007. Both Glaxo and Novartis obtained two approvals. Novartis has been among the leaders in obtaining new approvals in recent years.

Approval Date	Generic Name	Company	2006 R&D Budget
2/23/07	lisdexamfetamine dimesylate	New River	Unknown
03/03/07	Lapatinib Ditosylate	Glaxo Grp Ltd	~ $4 billion
03/05/07	Aliskiren Hemifumarate	Novartis	~ $5.3 billion
03 /16/07	Eculizumab	Alexion Pharm	83.225 million
04/12/07	Retapamulin	Glaxo Grp Ltd	~ $4 billion
05/09/07	Rotigotine	Schwarz Biosciences	€215.1 million
05/30/07	Temsirolimus	Wyeth Pharms Inc	~$3.1 billion
06/15/07	Ambrisentan	Gilead	~$384 million
08/06/07	Maraviroc	Pfizer	~$7.6 billion
08/23/07	Ammonia, N-13	Feinstein Institute for Medical Research	Unknown
08/30/07	Lanreotide Acetate	Beaufour Ipsen	€178.3
10/12/07	Doripenem	Johnson and Johnson	$7.125 billion
10/12/07	Raltegravir Potassium	Merck and Co, Inc	$4.783 billion
10/16/07	Ixabepilone	Bristol Myers Squibb	$3.067 billion
10/29/07	Nilotinib Hydrochloride Monohydrate	Novartis	~ $5.3 billion
11/14/07	methoxy polyethylene glycol-epoetin beta	Hoffman-LaRoche	CHF6.589 billion
12/13/07	Sapropterin Dihydrochloride	Biomarin	$66.735 million
12/17/07	Nebivolol	Mylan Bertek	$102.431 million[*]
12/27/07	6% Hydroxymethyl Starch in 0.9%NaCl Infusion	Fresenius Kabi	€167 million
12/27/07	6% Hydroxymethyl Starch in 0.9%NaCl Infusion	Fresenius Kabi	€167 million

[*]Note: Mylan is primarily a generic drug company, so presumably most of the R&D expense is associated with the development of generic drugs.

Two other products were approved by FDA in 2007, but they are not listed in the Table because they are not synthetic drugs, but rather, drugs prepared from animals or humans. These "biologics" are somewhat outside the scope of this book, which is oriented toward factory-manufactured drugs made from simple chemicals or produced by laboratory-grown cell systems.

Approval Date	Generic Name	Company
8/27/07	Human Thrombin Topical	Omrix Biopharmaceuticals, Ltd
3/30/07	Protein C Concentrate	Baxter Healthcare, Inc.

Companies that are able to get new drugs approved are generally good bets for long-term investors and as places to look for a job. Of course, if a company is large, it must get new products approved more quickly than it loses patent protections on existing products, or its revenues will fall over time. However, even when product approvals fall a bit behind patent expirations, a company's ability to get new products approved is a critical component of its long-term succes

Chapter 21 - A Final Cautionary Note

As I HOPE you now understand, successful drug development requires a complex mix of scientific and management abilities. In this section, I will try to briefly quantify the basic scientific skills needed to successfully manage development of a new chemical entity.

The following list summarizes the technical skills required for a good team leader.

- Basic inorganic and organic chemistry including stereochemistry
- A basic understanding of analytical chemistry including liquid chromatography, gas chromatography, mass spectrometry, thin layer chromatorgraphy, standard curves, and quality-control sampling
- A basic understanding of physical chemistry including solubility, polymorphs, and scanning calorimetry
- A basic understanding of biochemistry especially drug metabolism reactions

- An understanding of physiology including cardiac conduction, renal and hepatic excretion mechanisms, portal blood clearance of drugs, and enterohepatic recirculation
- A good understanding of electrocardiography, pulmonary, and renal function
- A basic understanding of toxicology study data including common adverse findings in control animals
- A good understanding of internal medicine - especially as it relates to drug adverse reactions and adverse health changes expected in various populations
- A good understanding of statistics, especially analysis of variance, corrections for multiple comparisons, and power calculations
- A good understanding of Good Clinical Practice Regulations, and a basic understanding of Good Laboratory Practice Regulations
- A basic understanding of drug metabolism
- A good understanding of pharmacokinetics, including hands-on experience doing pharmacokinetic calculations
- Sound management skills and experience managing complex tasks
- A strong physiology able to absorb psychic shocks.

What is difficult to convey is the level of scrutiny a new drug application will receive once it is submitted. As discussed earlier, patient numbers will be tallied various ways and all must add up consistently. The number of patients who complete the studies must equal the number enrolled minus the number who discontinue before the end of the study. The number of headaches, toothaches, strokes, etc. in the total database must exactly equal the sum of the number reported in the individual studies. Calculations of complex measures of drug absorption and elimination will be redone by the regulators and must match up exactly with the analysis submitted by the company sponsor. Finally, the whole new drug application must hold together and there can be no loose ends that suggest a flaw in the efficacy data or a possible risk which is not addressed in the risk-benefit analysis of the sponsor.

One might think that accomplishing this would be a matter of routine; however, this is far from the case. Data may come from published literature or experiments done by academic investigators, some of whom may also be working for competitors. Data will likely be available from studies done in foreign countries and submitted in languages the development team does not understand. All this must be tied together in a coherent analysis with no unaddressed ambiguities.

In my experience, companies often misinterpret data or report it in a misleading way. One of the more common errors is the unduly pessimistic interpretation of data. This kind of bias was contrary to the expectations I had when I first started working in drug development. As a young professional, I expected that to the extent data interpretations were slanted, they would be biased to make a product look better; safer or more effective than an impartial interpretation would reasonably support. Unduly optimistic data interpretation certainly does occur, especially in presentations to the public. However, inside a company it is more common to find data that suggests a possible risk being accepted at face value when a closer inspection would show that a methodological problem was the most likely explanation. I have seen this countless times. This kind of error is very dangerous because once an adverse finding is erroneously reported, it may be very difficult to correct with a new study. Even if the study is repeated and the adverse finding does not recur, the problem may not go away because then there are conflicting data: one study suggests a risk to patients and one does not. As might be expected, the regulators will be inclined to believe the study which suggests the risk and doubt the results of the study which did not replicate them. Furthermore, the inconsistency between the two results will raise justifiable doubts in the regulators' minds about the validity of other data generated by the sponsor. Thus, it may take many studies which don't show a risk in order to disprove one study that erroneously suggests a risk. This is the reason it is critically important to do things correctly the first time. Errors are often difficult or impossible to correct. Every calculation should be checked and all alternate interpretations of data should be considered.

I encountered what I believe was an erroneous report of an adverse finding early in my career. I was once told that a drug caused anemia, because during a study two dogs were noted to have a dramatic falls of blood hemoglobin. The hemoglobin eventually recovered in the face of continued drug administration but the observation of anemia was worrying. In reviewing the thousands of pages of appendices of the report of this study, I happened to notice that these two dogs, and only these two, had been involved in a fight with each other just before the decreased hemoglobin was observed. They both sustained wounds which caused bleeding. I suggested that the alternate explanation, decreased hemoglobin caused by bleeding from being bitten be included in the discussion of the study results. This proved to be a reasonable explanation, in later more carefully conducted studies when the animals were not injured no anemia was observed.

I have no way of knowing if adding the information about the dogfight helped the regulatory review of the product. However, I am confident that leaving out this potential explanation would have added unnecessary risk to the drug's approval and as explained in earlier parts of this book, reducing risk is the primary objective of the drug development professional.

When planning a drug-development project, always remember that the data being obtained will come from the dedicated, and the dishonest, the highly motivated and the depressed, the brilliant and the dolt, the altruistic and the malevolent, those who communicate well in your native language and those who think they do but really cannot. This data must all be analyzed using consistent standards, with errors corrected and bias removed. This is perhaps the most challenging part of drug development in the real world.

Acknowledgements

THIS BOOK WOULD not have been possible without the love and support of the four exceptional women in my life: my daughters, Emily, Jane, and Sarah, and my wife, Beth; they have made my life rich with their creative spirit, intellectual curiosity, and their "Can Do" attitudes. I'm especially grateful to Beth for her encouragement throughout the writing process, her invaluable comments on the readability of the manuscript as it evolved, and her editing prowess.

I would like to acknowledge the many people from ER Squibb Corporation who taught me, in their own brutal way, the proper approach to developing new drugs and paid me while doing so. It was the most cost-effective method of education I ever experienced.

I also want to recognize the contribution of the government employees around the world who regulate the development and marketing of new drugs. They enforce a sacred trust between pharmaceutical companies and the public; without their efforts, the average patient and physician would have to deal with a flood of dangerous products that would tarnish the entire pharmaceutical industry and interfere with the efficient delivery of healthcare. The approval system they have built over the last century, while not perfect, provides an enormous benefit to society.

Finally, I would like to thank my colleagues at Pharmaceutical Special Projects Group, LLC. I have learned more about drug development from them than I can calculate, especially as regards the human element, which is so vital to a successful development program.

Afterword

FOLLOWING COMPLETION OF this book, the FDA announced the availability of an analysis of the determinants of the success of companies at obtaining a rapid review and approval of their NDA's. A preview of the text of this report is available on the FDA website and is entitled "Independent Evaluation of FDA's First Cycle Review Performance – Retrospective Analysis Final Report." The analysis was based on NDA's for new chemical entities, although many of the conclusions would likely pertain to 505b2 applications as well. Of course, the analysis applies only to NDA's that were submitted to FDA; most products never make it to an NDA submission because of problems identified during the development process.

Even after the tremendous attrition that occurs during the pre-NDA drug development process, based on the report, it appears that overall, only 47% of submitted NDA's were approved on the first try; 23% were approved after one or more re-submissions, and the remaining 30% were not approved as of the end of the period examined (approximately 3 years).

The reasons FDA cited for failure to obtain "prompt approval" were equally distributed among safety, efficacy and manufacturing concerns.

The report supports the premise that products with a novel mechanism of action are more likely to be promptly approved than products with well-established, non-novel mechanisms of action (which are, most likely, similar to products that are already marketed); this bias would tend to offset the greater economic risks of failure during development for products that have novel mechanisms of action. For example, based on the report, a product with a novel mechanism of action that also targeted an acute, life-threatening condition had the highest likelihood of prompt approval (73%); and while a product with a novel mechanism of action that targeted a non-life-threatening condition was slightly less likely to achieve prompt approval (64%), the likelihood of its success is more than twice that of a product without a novel mechanism of action developed for a non-life-threatening disease (28%).

Overall, the report reflects that (i) in-licensed products were significantly more likely to succeed (65%) on the first submission than products discovered and developed within the same company, and (ii), when an NDA application is referred by the FDA for review by an FDA Advisory Committee, the chances for its first-time approval drop from 46% to 31%.

It is interesting and important to note that for FDA approvals, as in other spheres of human activities, "success begets success." The report strongly supports the contention that prior FDA approvals are a strong predictor of the chance that the submitting company's new product will be approved on its first submission. In fact, companies with a prior approval have a 51% chance of receiving approval on first submission, as opposed to a 30% chance for companies without a prior NDA approval. The benefit conferred by a prior approval applies even when such prior approval was obtained in a different therapeutic area (53%).

The results of this quantitative analysis are completely consistent with the strategies summarized in this book. In particular, they confirm the importance of using experienced staff who have a history of success in getting new products approved by FDA, maintaining strong internal controls of the drug-development process, and early and frequent communication with FDA. Since the reasons for failure to obtain rapid approval were found to be equally distributed among safety, efficacy and manufacturing concerns, it is important to have experienced staff in all three categories.

The report also confirms this book's emphasis on the importance of successful interactions with FDA prior to the commencement of phase III studies. A successful End-of-Phase II Meeting was identified as a good predictor of ultimate prompt approval of an NDA; this was attributed to the fact that once phase III studies are initiated, it becomes very difficult for companies to respond to FDA requests for changes, and therefore, in the absence of a successful End-of-Phase II Meeting, NDA applications are often submitted without adequate responses to FDA requests received after Phase III is underway.

It is worthy of note that a company's experience in getting a new product approved improves its chances of getting a second product approved, even if the second product is in a different therapeutic area. This suggests that success in getting a new product approved is attributable to a general understanding of the development process, rather than specific knowledge about the therapeutic area. Again, this is consistent with my experience. All of my NDA's have been successful, even though each was in a new therapeutic area in which I had essentially no prior experience. This is also consistent with the fact that the reasons for delayed or non-approvals are evenly distributed among safety, efficacy and manufacturing. Safety and manufacturing issues are usually similar across therapeutic areas, and therefore experience in one area is easily generalized to another.

Putting the results of the report together, the kind of product most likely to be promptly approved by FDA is one with a novel mechanism of action that targets an acute, life-threatening condition, has been through a successful End-of-Phase II Meeting, and is submitted by a company with a history of prior drug approvals.

Glossary

Adverse event – Any adverse change in a person's health. This includes symptoms that the patient complains of, or new adverse physical findings or laboratory test results. It may be a new event or a worsening of a prior condition. The adverse events of greatest importance in drug development are "treatment emergent adverse events", that is adverse events that emerge after treatment with an experimental medication has begun.

Blinded Study – A study in which some of the participants are not aware of which of the treatments being studied is administered to which study participant. In a single-blind study, the study participants are kept blinded. In a double-blind study, both the participants and the personnel implementing the study (including personnel within the pharmaceutical company sponsor) are kept blinded.

Clinical Hold – This is a letter from FDA responding to an IND application by refusing to let any clinical trials commence. It usually results in a long delay of development. A clinical hold is usually evidence of a significant problem in the company that submitted the IND, since it indicates the inability of the company to anticipate FDA's response to the IND submission.

Clinical Pharmacology – The study of the pharmacology of a drug in humans. In practice, this typically encompasses phase I studies of tolerability and pharmacokinetics, as well as evaluations of surrogate efficacy endpoints that may give insight into the likely efficacy that will be observed in later larger efficacy trials. Clinical pharmacology typically also includes evaluations of drug metabolism in humans, as well as the effects of various disease states (kidney or liver disease) and other drugs, foods, etc. on the absorption and elimination of a drug.

Compassionate Use Program – A study or group of studies that allows a drug that is still in development to be given to patients who urgently need it, but who may not qualify for inclusion in a formal evaluation of safety and efficacy. Much of the paperwork and other regulatory burdens of a regular study are still present in a compassionate use program; however, because of the less formal nature of the studies, the data collected are much less useful for obtaining regulatory approval than would be the case for a standard efficacy and safety study. Thus from the financial point of view, a compassionate use program is an expense without much of a balancing benefit. However, compassionate use programs may be required when it is unethical to withhold treatment from patients who urgently need it.

Complete Response Letter – A letter containing the results of the FDA's review of a New Drug Application; scheduled for 10 months after the NDA is submitted. The Complete Response letter lists the requirements for final approval of the new drug. This may consist solely of acceptance by the company of the FDA's proposed Package Insert language or may require extensive new analyses and/or data.

Consent Form – A form summarizing the risks and benefits of participating in a clinical study. Every participant in a clinical study must sign a consent form prior to participating in a clinical study. The form is typically prepared by the physician implementing the study and must be approved the Institutional Review or Ethics Committee responsible for the study and usually by the relevant government regulatory body (dependent on the country(s) where the study is conducted). The consent form is usually based on information contained in the Investigators' Brochure and study protocol document.

Debarment – FDA may debar a clinical investigator or other person for serious violations of laws or regulations. A debarred individual may not legally take part in the drug development process. Each new drug application must certify that no debarred individuals contributed to the application.

Degradant – An undesired substance that forms spontaneously during the storage of a drug.

ECG – Electrocardiogram. An assessment of electrical activity of the heart. Certain drug-induced changes of the ECG can be evidence of safety problems.

Effect Size – The size of the drug effect as measured by accepted techniques. Typically, the effect size is the difference between the effect of an active treatment and an inactive placebo treatment.

EKG – synonymous with ECG

EMEA – European Medicines Agency. The agency that regulates the pharmaceutical industry in the European Union. Each European country also has its own regulatory authority. The split of responsibilities between these national authorities and the EMEA is complex and has changed as the EU has evolved.

Ethics Committee – In Europe, a board of independent experts who evaluate the risks and benefits of a clinical study. They theoretically represent the interests of the patients. In practice, they are equally concerned with the potential legal liability of the institution where the study will be conducted.

Excipient – An inactive ingredient added to a drug product to enhance its physical characteristics or chemical stability. For example, the desired dose of a very active drug may be so small that the tablet could not be easily handled. In this case, an inactive ingredient could be added to increase its size.

Exploratory IND – A special type of IND application which allows very limited human studies and therefore requires less safety and efficacy information than a normal IND. Although this kind of application may be reasonable in certain very limited situations, its use may be a warning that the sponsor lacks the knowledge and/or resources to get a normal IND approved.

Exposure Multiple – The ratio of the exposure in animals to the exposure in humans. This may be calculated on a dose basis, e.g. mg of dose per kilogram body weight for the animal and mg per kilogram body weight in humans. It may also be calculated on a mg dose per square meter body surface area (which is believed to be a more accurate estimate of exposure), or it may be based on average blood drug levels (believed by many to be the most accurate estimate of exposure).

FDA – Food and Drug Administration. The part of the US Federal Government that regulates the drug industry.

Generic Drug – A drug approved under section 505j of the Food and Drug Law based on bioavailability data alone with no requirement for human safety or efficacy data.

Good Clinical Practice Guidelines – A set of FDA Guidance documents based on Good Clinical Practice Regulations. The FDA guidance documents can be found on the FDA website (http://www.fda.gov/oc/gcp/guidance.html). They specify procedures to be followed when conducting clinical investigations. These guidances are complex and failure to follow them can have dire consequences to both a company and individuals including invalidation of the results of a clinical study so that it must be repeated. Civil and/or criminal liability including debarment (see debarment, above) may also be a consequence of GCP violations.

Guidance Documents – These are documents issued by drug regulatory authorities. They are intended to give companies a general idea of the requirements for approval of a drug for marketing. They cover all aspects of drug development, including manufacturing, non-clinical testing, clinical studies, and drug marketing. They may be very specific, for example, limited to a specific disease or condition, or they may be very general relating to procedures for maintaining quality or records.

Half-Life – The half-life of a drug is the time it takes for the blood concentration to decrease by half. Most drugs are rapidly absorbed from the gastrointestinal tract and reach maximal levels in blood within 2 or 3 hours or administration. After reaching this peak, the blood levels typically decline with a relatively consistent half-life, first falling to one half the peak value, and then falling to one quarter and then one eighth over consecutive half-life intervals.

ICH – International Committee on Harmonization – A consortium formed to harmonize the drug approval requirements in the US, EU and Japan. Guidance documents issued by the ICH are accepted by regulators in all three territories.

Impurity – An undesired substance that forms during the manufacture of a drug.

IND Application – Investigational New Drug Application. This is an application for permission to administer a new drug to humans. It generally includes detailed information about the method of manufacture, safety and efficacy data from animal studies and proposed clinical studies. The FDA has 30 days to review an IND application. In the absence of objections from FDA, the proposed clinical investigations may proceed after the 30-day review period.

Institutional Review Board – In the US, a board of independent experts who evaluate the risks and benefits of a clinical study. They theoretically represent the interests of the patients. In practice they are equally concerned with the potential legal liability of the institution where the study will be conducted.

Investigators' Brochure – A document summarizing the known information about a drug product. It is used by the physicians participating in the human studies to judge the risks and benefits of enrolling patients in clinical trials.

Investigator-Sponsored IND – An IND submitted by a non-commercial sponsor, e.g. an academic researcher. Nominally, an investigator-sponsored IND must contain the same components as an IND for a commercial sponsor. However, in practice, the requirements for approval of an investigator sponsored IND are somewhat more lax. Thus, some companies will arrange for an investigator to submit an IND for their product. This raises the risk of problems, since the company gives up a significant measure of control of studies initiated under the IND and academic investigators are sometimes not skilled at drug development.

Koseisho – Ministry of Health and Welfare of Japan. This is the part of the Japanese government that regulates the pharmaceutical industry.

Lableled Adverse Events – These are events that are listed in the product's approved package insert or investigator's brochure which are supplied to the clinical investigators who run the clinical trials for a new drug and are the basis on which they determine the risk/benfit ratio for the trial. These documents are also used to make up the consent forms that patients must sign before they are allowed to enroll in a clinical trial.

Linear – Two things are said to have a linear relationship when they change in proportion to one another. If the levels of drug found in blood change in proportion to the administered dose, then the drug is said to have linear pharmacokinetics. Most drugs have linear pharmacokinetics. Non-linear pharmacokinetics can occur when the absorption or elimination of a drug can be saturated by high doses.

Misbranded Drug – A drug that is marketed outside of the conditions of regulatory approval. A drug may become misbranded because the actual drug product is changed in some way without regulatory approval. A drug may also become misbranded because it is marketed using promotional materials that are outside the approved Package Insert.

MRI – Magnetic Resonance Imaging. A method for visualizing the internal structure of the living body based on the differences in electromagnetic properties of different tissues.

NDC Code – National Drug Code. This is a unique code number for each drug product marketed in the United States.

Pivotal Study – A study designed to satisfy the regulatory requirements for demonstrating efficacy in humans. Pivotal efficacy studies are often the most expensive, and time-consuming part of the drug development process and the most susceptible to unexpected problems. They are also the most carefully scrutinized by regulators.

Power calculation – A calculation of the chance for a study to succeed. The calculation is based on the expected size of the drug effect (e.g. difference between active drug and placebo) and the variability of the effect. The study power is usually expressed as the percentage chance that the study will show efficacy, if the drug is really as effective and variable as expected. Power calculations can also be used to estimate the ability of a study to detect a safety problem based on its expected rate of occurrence.

Pro-drug – An inactive substance that is converted to an active drug after being administered.

Protocol – A document outlining, in great detail, the procedures to be used when conducting an experimental study. Protocols for human studies usually must be approved by Institutional Review or Ethics Committees prior to implementation. They are also reviewed by regulatory authorities, although not always in advance of implementation.

Serious Adverse Event – An event that results in death, is life-threatening results in permanent disability or that requires or extends hospitalization. An event that requires treatment to avoid the previously listed outcomes also qualifies as serious.

Toxicology Species – The animal species used in relatively standardized assessments of drug safety. Typically a rodent (mouse or rat) and a non-rodent species (dog) are used.

Treatment Emergent Signs and Symptoms – Signs or symptoms that occur or worsen after treatment with a drug product has started. Symptoms are problems reported by the patient while signs are noted by an outside observer. These are the events tracked during drug development and reported in the Package Insert. Adverse events that begin prior to, and do not worsen during, treatment are generally classified as pre-existing conditions and are assumed to be unrelated to treatment with the experimental drug.

Unexpected Adverse Event – An adverse event that is not listed in the product package insert or investigators brochure.

USAN – United States Adopted Names Council. The organization that assigns generic names to new molecular entities.

Warning Letter – A letter from the FDA warning a company of a serous regulatory problem. Such letters are a matter of public record. Issuance of a warning letter is typically (though not always) preceded by other, non-publicly disclosed citations by FDA inspectors. Therefore, in most cases competent companies can avoid the issuance of warning letters by fixing problems before they reach the warning-letter stage. Failure to adequately fix problems in a warning letter may result in punitive actions by FDA up to and including: seizure of product, closure of manufacturing facilities and/or prohibition of drug shipments.

Appendix 1 - Types of New Drug Applications

505b1 - APPLICATIONS for permission to market a new drug fall into three major categories, derived from the regulations that cover drug approval. This book has described the process used to get a drug product containing a new molecule approved. This approval procedure is governed by the regulations in Section 505b1 of the Food and Drug Law and which required submission of all the information needed for the FDA to judge the safety and efficacy of the product proposed for marketing approval.

505j - This is an application to market a "generic" form of a drug that has already been approved as a new drug under 505b1. A company applying for approval of a generic drug is not required to supply a complete data package for its product; instead it is allowed to "rely" data already on file for the innovator product approved under Section 505b1. The generic company is allowed to use the data developed by the innovator company, even though the innovator company has not granted it permission to use its data.

In general, the generic product can be approved based only on information regarding its method of manufacture and the drug blood levels it produces when the product is administered to healthy volunteers. To be approved, the generics must reproduce closely the average blood levels produced by the innovator product. The criteria for how close the match must be are specified in the relevant FDA guidance (Bioavailability and Bioequivalence Studies for Orally Administered Drug Products - General Considerations, March 2003).

In order to qualify as a generic, the product must be the same dose form (e.g. tablet, solution, etc.), contain exactly the same active ingredient, and be given using the same dose regimen.

505b2 - Products that are not completely new but that don't qualify as generics can still be approved under the 505b2 regulations. These are products whose approval relies to some degree on data filed at FDA by an innovator company, but that differ from the innovator product in a way that prevents them from qualifying for approval as a generic. For example, a new dose form may qualify for approval under the 505b2 regulations. Frequently, such new dose forms use controlled-release technology to reduce the number of daily doses and thus increase convenience for patients. The new dose regimen means the product does not qualify as a generic.

New Biologics - Biologic drugs are made from natural products or living tissues, and therefore tend to have much more complicated chemical structures than drugs synthesized using standard chemical techniques. Furthermore, biologics are often mixtures of several or many different components. Because of these differences from chemically synthesized drugs, biologics are approved based on somewhat different procedures from those used for drugs that are synthesized using more chemical methods. In particular, the manufacturing requirements are often quite different, especially for products that are mixtures of many ingredients. FDA is currently considering what will be required for a generic biologic to gain approval. However, for the moment, most biologics are not subject to generic competition in the US. The European Agency has begun to approve generic forms of biologic drugs.

Orphan Drug - An "orphan drug" is defined as a drug designed to treat a condition which affects no more than 200,000 people in the US (in the EU the definition is similar). The drug laws provide special benefits to companies that develop orphan drugs. Primarily, they have much stronger protection from other potentially competitive drugs by granting exclusivity for 7 years. Many orphan drugs are very profitable, because the limits on competition allow a company to charge very high prices for an orphan product. Furthermore, because the potential patient population is usually small, the required development program may be much smaller and faster than for a regular indication. Some orphan drugs have been approved based on data from less than 100 patients. Orphan drugs may be approved under regulation 505b1 or 505b2, depending on the type of data required for approval.

Sub-part H Approvals - Sub-part H of the regulations allows a product to be approved based on "surrogate" efficacy endpoints. These are assessments of efficacy that may be easier or faster to measure than the standard endpoints normally required for approval of a new drug. As a condition of approval under sub-part H, a company will typically be required to provide standard efficacy evaluations following approval. In order to assure that a company really does supply the extra efficacy data, the FDA typically requires that the studies using standard efficacy endpoints be well underway at the time approval is granted based on the surrogate endpoints. In addition, the requirements for approval using surrogate endpoints are typically much more rigorous than would be required for a normal NDA. Thus, approval under sub-part H does not usually accelerate a drug development program, and may actually take longer than the normal NDA process. My advice is to think carefully about approval under sub-part H. It sounds like a good idea but in practice it often isn't. Sub-part H approvals may be granted under regulations 505b1 or 505b2.

Fast Track Designation - A product may qualify for Fast-Track Designation if it fulfills an important unmet medical need. Theoretically, this designation can be applied for at any stage of development, starting with the initial IND submission. This designation qualifies the product for special attention and expedited reviews. As a practical matter, FDA is not likely to grant a fast-track designation to a product until there is a reasonable expectation that it will be successfully developed for a serious unmet medical need, and this is usually not fulfilled until well after the initial IND submission. Fast-track designation is important because it allows better coordination of the development program with FDA and faster turnaround on regulatory submissions. It also suggests that should the product be approved, it will be easy and cheap to market since there will be little to no competition. However, when fast-track is granted to a truly novel product, it only partially offsets the additional risks associated with very novel, therapies so a fast-track designation should not be interpreted as an indication that the development program is low risk.

Approvals in the European Union, Canada and Australia — A detailed description of these approval processes is beyond the scope of this book. However, the process is generally similar to the US procedure and equivalents of the 505b1, 505b2 and 505j approvals exist in most other countries.

Approvals in Small Countries - Small countries often lack the government infrastructure to do sophisticated new drug application reviews. So, they will often accept approval in the US or EU as a basis for their approval. Thus, approval in the US or EU will automatically qualify a product for approval in many small country markets.

Each of these types of new drug approvals is generally associated with a period of marketing exclusivity. The periods vary depending on the type of approval and the country. Important exclusivity periods in the US are summarized in the following table.

Some Exclusivity Periods Granted in the United States				
Approval	Basis for Exclusivity	Duration	Comment	
505b1	New molecular entity	5 years	Runs concurrently with patent protection.	
505b2	New formulation	3 years	Blocks generics but not other 505b2 approvals. Runs concurrently with patent protection.	
505j	First to file	6 months	Blocks approval of generics of the same drug product. Runs concurrently with patent protection.	
Pediatric	Study of use in pediatric patients	6 months	Adds to duration of patent protection.	

This table summarizes the simplest forms of exclusivity. However, exclusivity is a very complex subject. The reader is advised to obtain professional assistance for specific situations. It is also important to remember that the duration of patent protection for a drug is often adjusted to compensate for the period required to do drug development. This is also a complex but very important subject. The durations of exclusivity and patent protection for approved products can be found on the FDA website in the "Electronic Orange Book" which may be found at http://www.fda.gov/cder/ob/default.htm.

Appendix 2 - Inside Info: Open Secrets in the Pharmaceutical Industry

1. MOST PEOPLE are surprised to learn that the FDA cannot revoke the approval of a product. Once approved, a product remains approved forever, even if terrible toxicity is discovered after the approval is granted and even if the data submitted to support the approval are found to be fraudulent and/or erroneous. When significant problems arise post-approval, the FDA can only pressure a sponsor to remove the product from the market. FDA has various tools it can use to apply such pressure: for example, it can issue a warning to the public, which makes the company selling the product liable to lawsuits by injured consumers. Also, FDA can compel a sponsor to include onerous language in the product's package insert that would dissuade physicians and patients from using the product. Either of these approaches can essentially force a company to remove a dangerous product from the market. However, since the FDA cannot absolutely compel a company to remove its product from the market, when problems

occur, products tend to remain on the market longer than they probably should.

2. Most people understand that generic products do not go through the same approval process as their related innovator products. This is sometimes interpreted as implying that branded products are superior to generics and to impugn the process used to approve generics as being not sufficiently rigorous. However, the same bioequivalence evaluation used to gain approval of a generic drug is often used as part of the development of branded (non-generic) drugs. For example, when an innovator company makes a small change in a product, the new, changed product is often approved based on the same criteria used to approve generics, rather than repeating the entire development program. Such small changes are very common in the pharmaceutical business. For example, as discussed earlier, a small-scale manufacturing process is generally used early in development of a new product, because production runs need only supply small studies. Once the product is approved for marketing, manufacturing will generally need to be scaled up many-fold to manufacture the quantities needed in the market. Generally the changes made during the scale-up of the manufacturing process are sufficiently large that the manufacturer cannot guarantee that the large-scale product is really identical to the product used in the clinical and other trials. In this common situation, the innovator company conducts a study to show that the scaled up commercial product produces the same blood drug levels as the product used in the clinical trials. The criteria for showing equivalence are the same as those used to show the equivalence of brand and generics products. In this sense, even innovator products are usually "generic" equivalents of the products used in the clinical trials.

3. The high cost of drugs is not due to the cost of development. Large pharmaceutical companies spend much more money marketing drugs than they spend discovering and developing new ones. This makes short-term sense because marketing expenditures often result in a quick payback, while money spent discovering and developing new drugs will only generate money in the more distant future or perhaps, not at all. Even the money spent discovering and developing new drugs is largely spent on products that fail during development. This is often attributed to the "high risk" of drug discovery and development. However, this notion of high risk cannot be accepted uncritically. Drug discovery and development is no more inherently "high risk" than any other business venture. Some projects are very risky and others have less risk. The trick is to be sure that the risks are balanced by potential rewards, and that a company's portfolio contains a reasonable balance of low and high-risk projects, so that a reliable flow of regulatory approvals is maintained. This can be done with superior management and highly productive personnel. However, the idea the drug development is high risk is difficult to dispel, in part because the investment community has accepted the idea that failure is common and therefore a high success rate is impossible.

4. It seems increasingly common that we hear news reports of problems with adverse events that occur after a product is approved for marketing. What's the story? Why is this happening?

As discussed throughout this book, drug development is an exercise in risk management. This book has examined it from the point of view of a company developing a new product. However, the drug regulators face the same issues. How much safety data should they require? If they increase the requirements, the products they approve will produce fewer nasty surprises. However, the increased time and financial burden on pharmaceutical companies will mean fewer products will be developed, and their approvals will be delayed because of the extra time required to collect additional safety information. Conversely, lowering requirements will result in more products being available, but a higher risk of post-marketing problems. This dilemma is common in setting government policy and ultimately, it must be settled by a political process responding to societal pressures and concerns.

As discussed in Chapter 19, the last changes to the Food and Drug law lowered the requirements for marketing approval. So where are we now? The current requirements are summarized quite succinctly in the relevant FDA Guidance (Guidance for Industry, Premarketing Risk Assessment, May 2004). Among other requirements, it states that, at a minimum, an NDA database for a drug used chronically, must include at least 1,500 patients who have received multiple doses, of which 300-600 patients must be treated for 6 months, and at least 100 patients treated for 1 year, all at doses "relevant" to those proposed for marketing.

According to the FDA's calculations (Guideline for Industry, The Extent of Population Exposure to Assess Clinical Safety: For Drugs Intended for Long-Term Treatment of Non-Life-Threatening Conditions, March 1995), these patient numbers should allow detection of adverse events that occur in 0.5% to 5% of patients during a six-month period, or in 3% or more of patients during one year of exposure. In general, there is no requirement for data from patients treated for more than one year. These requirements were developed over many years after extensive consultation with many experts and have, in my opinion, achieved a reasonable balance between development cost and patient safety, especially because companies generally exceed these minimum requirements by significant margins.

However, the requirements have clear limitations. They cannot reliably detect adverse events occurring in less that 0.5% of patients during six months, or less than 3% of patients during one year of treatment. Since data beyond one year is generally not required, events that take more than one year will not be detected at all.

Because of these limitations, one must expect that in some cases, relatively rare and/or delayed adverse events will not be observed during the NDA development process. This should be kept in mind by patients when thought is given to using newly-approved products. Although beyond the scope of this book, safety assessments continue after a product is approved, and in some cases new risks will be identified when the product is used by millions of patients for a number of years. Such uncommon risks simply can't be reliably identified in advance using the current approval criteria. For this reason, it is often prudent for patients to wait two or three years after a product is approved before trying it, if acceptable alternatives are available.

Appendix 3 - FDA Non-Clinical Guidance Document

GUIDANCE FOR INDUSTRY

**M3 Nonclinical Safety Studies
for the Conduct of Human Clinical
Trials for Pharmaceuticals
July 1997
ICH**

GUIDANCE FOR INDUSTRY

M3 Nonclinical Safety Studies for the Conduct of Human Clinical Trials for Pharmaceuticals

Additional copies are available from:
the Drug Information Branch (HFD-21O),
Center for Drug Evaluation and Research (CDER),
5600 Fishers Lane, Rockville, MD 20857 (Tel) 301-827-4573
http://www.fda.gov/cder/guidance/index.htm
or
Office of Communication,
Training, and Manufacturers Assistance (HFM-40)
Center for Biologics Evaluation and Research (CBER)
1401 Rockville Pike, Rockville, MD 20852-1448,
http://www.fda.gov/cber/guidelines.htm

(Fax) 888-CBERFAX or 301-827-3844
(Voice Information) 800-835-4709 or 301-827-1800

U.S. Department of Health and Human Services
Food and Drug Administration
Center for Drug Evaluation and Research (CDER)
Center for Biologics Evaluation and Research (CBER)
July 1997
ICH

Table of Contents

GUIDANCE FOR INDUSTRY[1]

M3 Nonclinical Safety Studies for the Conduct of Human Clinical Trials for Pharmaceuticals

I. INTRODUCTION (1)

A.   Objectives of the Guidance (1.1)

The purpose of this document is to recommend international standards for and to promote harmonization of the nonclinical

---

[1] This guidance was developed within the Expert Working Group (Multidisciplinary (Safety/Efficacy)) of the International Conference on Harmonisation of Technical Requirements for Registration of Pharmaceuticals for Human Use (ICH) and has been subject to consultation by the regulatory parties, in accordance with the ICH process. This document has been endorsed by the ICH Steering Committee at Step 4 of the ICH process, July 1997. At Step 4 of the process, the final draft is recommended for adoption to the regulatory bodies of the European Union, Japan and the United States. This guidance was published in the Federal Register on November 25, 1997 (62 FR 62922), and is applicable to drug and biological products. This guidance represents the Agency's current thinking on nonclinical safety studies for the conduct of human clinical trials for pharmaceuticals. It does not create or confer any rights for or on any person and does not operate to bind FDA or the public. An alternative approach may be used if such approach satisfies the requirements of the applicable statute, regulations, or both.

safety studies needed to support human clinical trials of a given scope and duration.

Harmonization of the guidance for nonclinical safety studies will help to define the current recommendations and reduce the likelihood that substantial differences will exist between regions.

This guidance should facilitate the timely conduct of clinical trials and reduce the unnecessary use of animals and other resources. This should promote safe and ethical development and availability of new pharmaceuticals.

B.   Background (1.2)

The recommendations for the extent of nonclinical safety studies to support the various stages of clinical development differ among the regions of Europe, the United States, and Japan. This raises the important question of whether there is scientific justification for these differences and whether it would be possible to develop a mutually acceptable guidance.

The present guidance represents the consensus that exists among the ICH regions regarding the scope and duration of nonclinical safety studies to support the conduct of human clinical trials for pharmaceuticals.

C.   Scope of the Guidance (1.3)

The nonclinical safety study recommendations for the marketing approval of a pharmaceutical usually include single and repeated dose toxicity studies, reproduction toxicity studies, genotoxicity studies, local tolerance studies, and for drugs that have special cause for concern or are intended for a long duration of use, an assessment of carcinogenic potential. Other nonclinical studies include pharmacology studies for safety assessment (safety pharmacology) and pharmacokinetic (absorption, distribution, metabolism, and excretion (ADME)) studies. These types of studies and their relation to the conduct of human clinical trials are presented in this guidance.

This guidance applies to the situations usually encountered during the conventional development of pharmaceuticals and should be viewed as providing general guidance for drug development. Animal safety studies and human clinical trials should be planned and designed to represent an approach that is scientifically and ethically appropriate for the pharmaceutical under development.

There have been marked changes in the kinds of therapeutic agents being developed (e.g., biotechnology-derived products), and the existing paradigms for safety evaluation may not always be appropriate or relevant. The safety evaluation in such cases should be considered on a case-by-case basis as described in the ICH guidance "Safety Studies in Biotechnological Products" (Ref. 1). Similarly, pharmaceuticals under development for indications in life-threatening or serious diseases without current effective therapy may also warrant a case-by-case approach to both the toxicological evaluation and clinical development to optimize and expedite drug development. In these cases, particular studies may be abbreviated, deferred, or omitted.

D.   General Principles (1.4)

The development of a pharmaceutical is a stepwise process involving an evaluation of both the animal and human safety information. The goals of the nonclinical safety evaluation include: A characterization of toxic effects with respect to target organs, dose dependence, relationship to exposure, and potential reversibility. This information is important for the estimation of an initial safe starting dose for the human trials and the identification of parameters for clinical monitoring for potential adverse effects. The nonclinical safety studies, although limited at the beginning of clinical development, should be adequate to characterize potential toxic effects under the conditions of the supported clinical trial.

Human clinical trials are conducted to demonstrate the efficacy and safety of a pharmaceutical, starting with a relatively low exposure in a small number of subjects. This is followed by clinical trials in which exposure usually increases by dose, duration, and/or size of the exposed patient population. Clinical trials are extended based on the demonstration of adequate safety in the previous clinical trial(s) as well as additional nonclinical safety information that is available as the clinical trials proceed. Serious adverse clinical or nonclinical findings may influence the continuation of clinical trials and/or suggest the need for additional nonclinical studies and a reevaluation of previous clinical adverse events to resolve the issue.

Clinical trials are conducted in phases for which different terminology has been utilized in the various regions. This document uses the terminology as defined in the ICH guidance "General Considerations for Clinical Trials" (Ref. 2). Clinical trials may be grouped by their purpose and objectives. The first human exposure studies are generally single dose studies, followed by dose escalation and short-term repeated dose studies to evaluate pharmacokinetic parameters and tolerance (Phase I studies - Human Pharmacology studies). These studies are often conducted in healthy volunteers but may also include patients. The next phase of trials consists of exploratory efficacy and safety studies in patients (Phase II studies - Therapeutic Exploratory studies). This is followed by confirmatory clinical trials for efficacy and safety in patient populations (Phase III studies - Therapeutic Confirmatory studies).

II.   SAFETY PHARMACOLOGY (2)

Safety pharmacology includes the assessment of effects on vital functions, such as cardiovascular, central nervous, and respiratory systems, and these should be evaluated prior to human exposure. These evaluations may be conducted as additions to toxicity studies or as separate studies.

III.   TOXICOKINETIC AND PHARMACOKINETIC STUDIES (3)

Exposure data in animals should be evaluated prior to human clinical trials (Ref. 3). Further information on ADME in animals should be made available to compare human and animal metabolic pathways. Appropriate information should usually be available by the time the Phase I (Human Pharmacology) studies have been completed.

IV.   SINGLE DOSE TOXICITY STUDIES (4)

The single dose (acute) toxicity for a pharmaceutical should be evaluated in two mammalian species prior to the first human exposure (Note 1). A dose escalation study is considered an acceptable alternative to the single dose design.

V. REPEATED DOSE TOXICITY STUDIES (5)

The recommended duration of the repeated dose toxicity studies is usually related to the duration, therapeutic indication, and scale of the proposed clinical trial. In principle, the duration of the animal toxicity studies conducted in two mammalian species (one nonrodent) should be equal to or exceed the duration of the human clinical trials up to the maximum recommended duration of the repeated dose toxicity studies (Tables 1 and 2).

In certain circumstances, where significant therapeutic gain has been shown, trials may be extended beyond the duration of supportive repeated dose toxicity studies on a case-by-case basis.

A. Phase I and II Studies (5.1)

A repeated dose toxicity study in two species (one nonrodent) for a minimum duration of 2-4 weeks (Table 1) would support Phase I (Human Pharmacology) and Phase II (Therapeutic Exploratory) studies up to 2 weeks in duration. Beyond this, 1-,3-, or 6-month toxicity studies would support these types of human clinical trials for up to 1, 3, or 6 months, respectively. Six-month rodent and chronic nonrodent studies (Ref. 11) would support clinical trials of longer duration than 6 months.

Table 1. Duration of Repeated Dose Toxicity Studies to Support Phase I and II Trials in the EU and Phase I, II, and III Trials in the United States and Japan[1]

Duration of Clinical Trials	Minimum Duration of Repeated Dose Toxicity Studies	
	Rodents	Non Rodents
Single dose	2-4 Weeks[2]	2 Weeks
Up to 2 Weeks	2-4 Weeks[2]	2 Weeks
Up to 1 Month	1 Month	1 Month
Up to 3 Months	3 Months	3 Months
Up to 6 Months	6 Months	6 Months[3]
>6 Months	6 Months	Chronic[3]

1 In Japan, if there are no Phase II clinical trials of equivalent duration to the planned Phase III trials, conduct of longer duration toxicity studies should be considered as given in Table 2.

2 In the EU and the United States, 2-week studies are the minimum duration. In Japan, 2-week nonrodent and 4-week rodent studies are needed (Also see Note 2). In the United States, as an alternative to 2-week studies, single dose toxicity studies with extended examinations can support single dose human trials (Ref. 4).

3 See Ref. 11. Data from 6 months of administration in nonrodents should be available before the initiation of clinical trials longer than 3 months. Alternatively, if applicable, data from a 9-month nonrodent study should be available before the treatment duration exceeds that which is supported by the available toxicity studies.

B. Phase III Studies (5.2)

For the Phase III (Therapeutic Confirmatory) studies, the recommendations for the United States and Japan are the same as those in Table 1. In the EU, a 1-month toxicity study in two species (one nonrodent) would support clinical trials of up to 2 weeks duration (Table 2). Three-month toxicity studies would support clinical trials for up to 1 month duration, while 6-month toxicity studies in rodents and 3-month studies in nonrodents would support clinical trials of a duration up to 3 months. For longer term clinical trials, a 6-month study in rodents and a chronic study in nonrodents are recommended.

Table 2. Duration of Repeated Dose Toxicity Studies to Support Phase III Trials in the EU and Marketing in All Regions[1]

Duration of Clinical Trials	Minimum Duration of Repeated Dose Toxicity Studies	
	Rodents	Non Rodents
Up to 2 Weeks	1 Month	1 Month
Up to 1 Month	3 Months	3 Months
Up to 3 Months	6 Months	3 Months
> 3 Months	6 Months	Chronic2

1 The above table also reflects the marketing recommendations in the three regions except that a chronic nonrodent study is recommended for clinical use > 1 month.

2 See Ref. 11.

VI. LOCAL TOLERANCE STUDIES (6)

Local tolerance should be studied in animals using routes relevant to the proposed clinical administration. The evaluation of local tolerance should be performed prior to human exposure. The assessment of local tolerance may be part of other toxicity studies.

VII. GENOTOXICITY STUDIES (7)

Prior to first human exposure, in vitro tests for the evaluation of mutations and chromosomal damage are generally needed. If an equivocal or positive finding occurs, additional testing should be performed (Ref. 5).

The standard battery of tests for genotoxicity (Ref. 6) should be completed prior to the initiation of Phase II studies.

VIII. CARCINOGENICITY STUDIES (8)

Completed carcinogenicity studies are not usually needed in advance of the conduct of clinical trials unless there is cause for concern. Conditions relevant for carcinogenicity testing are discussed in the ICH document (Ref. 7).

For pharmaceuticals developed to treat certain serious diseases, carcinogenicity testing, if needed, may be concluded postapproval.

IX. REPRODUCTION TOXICITY STUDIES (9)

Reproduction toxicity studies (Refs. 8 and 9) should be conducted as is appropriate for the population that is to be exposed.

A. Men (9.1)

Men may be included in Phase I and II trials prior to the conduct of the male fertility study since an evaluation of the male reproductive organs is performed in the repeated dose toxicity studies (Note 2).

A male fertility study should be completed prior to the initiation of Phase III trials (Refs. 8 and 9).

B. Women Not of Childbearing Potential (9.2)

Women not of childbearing potential (i.e., permanently sterilized, postmenopausal) may be included in clinical trials without reproduction toxicity studies provided the relevant repeated dose toxicity studies (which include an evaluation of the female reproductive organs) have been conducted.

C. Women of Childbearing Potential (9.3)

For women of childbearing potential there is a high level of concern for the unintentional exposure of an embryo/fetus before information is available concerning the potential benefits versus potential risks. There are currently regional differences in the timing of reproduction toxicity studies to support the inclusion of women of childbearing potential in clinical trials.

In Japan, assessment of female fertility and embryo-fetal development should be completed prior to the inclusion of women of childbearing potential using birth control in any type of clinical trial. In the EU, assessment of embryo-fetal development should be completed prior to Phase I trials in women of childbearing potential and female fertility studies prior to Phase III trials.

In the United States, women of childbearing potential may be included in early, carefully monitored studies without reproduction toxicity studies provided appropriate precautions are taken to minimize risk. These precautions include pregnancy testing (for example, based on the b-subunit of HCG), use of a highly effective method of birth control (Note 3), and entry after a confirmed menstrual period. Continued testing and monitoring during the trial should be sufficient to ensure compliance with the measures not to become pregnant during the period of drug exposure (which may exceed the length of study). To support this approach, informed consent should include any known pertinent information related to reproductive toxicity, such as a general assessment of potential toxicity of pharmaceuticals with related structures or pharmacological effects. If no relevant information is available, the informed consent should clearly note the potential for risk.

In the United States, assessment of female fertility and embryo-fetal development should be completed before women of childbearing potential using birth control are enrolled in Phase III trials.

In the three regions, the pre- and postnatal development study should be submitted for marketing approval or earlier if there is cause for concern. For all regions, all female reproduction toxicity studies (Ref. 8) and the standard battery of genotoxicity tests (Ref. 6) should be completed prior to the inclusion, in any clinical trial, of women of childbearing potential not using highly effective birth control (Note 3) or whose pregnancy status is unknown.

D. Pregnant Women (9.4)

Prior to the inclusion of pregnant women in clinical trials, all the reproduction toxicity studies (Refs. 8 and 9) and the standard battery of genotoxicity tests (Ref. 6) should be conducted. In addition, safety data from previous human exposure are generally needed.

X. SUPPLEMENTARY STUDIES (10)

Additional nonclinical studies may be needed if previous nonclinical or clinical findings with the product or related products have indicated special safety concerns.

XI. CLINICAL TRIALS IN PEDIATRIC POPULATIONS (11)

When pediatric patients are included in clinical trials, safety data from previous adult human exposure would usually represent the most relevant information and should generally be available before pediatric clinical trials. The necessity for adult human data would be determined on a case-by-case basis.

In addition to appropriate repeated dose toxicity studies, all reproduction toxicity studies (Ref. 8) and the standard battery of genotoxicity tests (Ref. 6) should be available prior to the initiation of trials in pediatric populations. Juvenile animal studies should be considered on an individual basis when previous animal data and human safety data are insufficient.

The need for carcinogenicity testing should be addressed prior to long term exposure in pediatric clinical trials considering the length of treatment or cause for concern (Ref. 7).

XII.   CONTINUING EFFORTS TO IMPROVE HARMONIZATION (12)

It is recognized that significant advances in harmonization of the timing of nonclinical safety studies for the conduct of human clinical trials for pharmaceuticals have already been achieved and are detailed in this guidance. However, differences remain in a few areas. These include toxicity studies to support first entry into man and the recommendations for reproduction toxicity studies for women of childbearing potential. Regulators and industry will continue to consider these differences and work towards further improving the drug development process.

XIII. ENDNOTES (13)

Note 1 For the conduct of single dose toxicity studies, refer to the ICH-l recommendations (Ref. 10) and the regional guidances.

Note 2 There are currently regional differences for the minimum duration of repeated dose toxicity studies; 2 weeks in the EU and the United States, and 2 weeks nonrodent and 4 weeks rodent in Japan. In Japan, unlike the EU and the United States, the male fertility study has usually been conducted prior to the inclusion of men in clinical trials. However, an assessment of male fertility by careful histopathological examination in the rodent 4-week repeated dose toxicity study has been found to be more sensitive in detecting effects on male reproductive organs than fertility studies (Ref. 9), and is now recommended to be performed prior to the first clinical trial in Japan. In the EU and the United States, 2-week repeated dose studies are considered adequate for an overall assessment of the potential toxicity of a drug to support clinical trials for a short duration.

Note 3 A highly effective method of birth control is defined as one that results in a low failure rate (i.e., less than 1 percent per year) when used consistently and correctly, such as implants, injectables, combined oral contraceptives, some intrauterine contraceptive devices (IUDs), sexual abstinence, or a vasectomized partner. For subjects using a hormonal contraceptive method, information regarding the product under evaluation and its potential effect on the contraceptive should be addressed.

XIV. REFERENCES (14)

1. ICH Topic S6 Document "Preclinical Testing of Biotechnology-Derived Pharmaceuticals."

2. ICH Topic E8 Document "General Considerations for Clinical Trials."

3. ICH Harmonised Tripartite Guideline (S3A) Note for "Toxicokinetics: The Assessment of Systemic Exposure in Toxicity Studies."

4. FDA, "Single Dose Acute Toxicity Testing for Pharmaceuticals; Revised Guidance," 61 FR 43934 to 43935, August 26,1996.

5. ICH Harmonised Tripartite Guideline (S2A) "Guidance on Specific Aspects of Regulatory Genotoxicity Tests."

6. ICH Topic S2B document "Standard Battery of Genotoxicity Tests."

7. ICH Harmonised Tripartite Guideline (S1A) "Guideline on the Need for Carcinogenicity Studies for Pharmaceuticals."

8. ICH Harmonised Tripartite Guideline (S5A) "Detection of Toxicity to Reproduction for Medicinal Products."

9. ICH Harmonised Tripartite Guideline (S5B) "Toxicity to Male Fertility."

10. Arcy, P. F., and D. W. G. Harron, "Proceeding of The First International Conference on Harmonisation, Brussels 1991," Queen's University of Belfast, pp 183-184 (1992).

11. ICH Topic S4 Document "Duration of Chronic Toxicity Testing in Animals (Rodent and Nonrodent Toxicity Testing)."

Appendix 4 - Brief Discussion of Manufacturing Issues

Drug development requires manufacturing of the drug product to be tested and ultimately marketed. Data from many clinical and animal studies will ultimately be integrated together in the documents submitted to government regulators for review and approval. To be successful, this data integration must take into account variations of the product during the process of development.

Ideally, the product tested in every study should be identical; however, in practice, this rarely happens. For example, as development proceeds, the active drug substance and dose form must be manufactured at larger and larger scales. This scale-up can introduce variations in the drug substance or product that can confound interpretation of the ultimate regulatory submission. Thus, it is critical to monitor the drug substance and product for variations during development, to be sure that they do not complicate the ultimate interpretation of the regulatory submission.

In general, the only changes in the manufacturing method that should be permitted are "improvements" in the drug substance and product, such as a change that reduces the level of an impurity, or a change that improves the reliability of the manufacturing process.

It is often necessary to prove that the scale up of the manufacturing process required for commercial production does not affect the absorption of the active drug substance. This typically is done via assessments of the blood levels of the active drug following administration of both the small scale and large scale manufactured product. Although these studies are not complicated, they do take time and can sometimes fail initially; then they must be repeated after the manufacturing process is fixed. Thus, adequate resources and time should be allocated to completing the appropriate studies prior to submission of the marketing application.

For an NDA to be approved, it is necessary to have data showing that the product and active drug substance have adequate stability in the packaging that will be used for the marketed product. Usually, at least 6 months of real-time stability data at room temperature are required along with additional data accumulated under more stressful conditions (higher temperature, humidity, etc.). Again, it is important to include time and resources for these stability assessments in the development plan. Stability data on batches made at a commercial scale will be required for the marketing approval.

A discussion of "release specifications" is beyond the scope of this book. However, the drug developer will hear the term from time to time. Suffice it to say that release specifications affect the quality of the drug substance and product and therefore should generally remain the same or be tightened as the drug development process proceeds. Any mention of loosening specifications should be viewed with extreme caution. Discussion of such loosening with regulators, prior to implementation, is usually warranted.

One additional item that is often ambiguous and requires detailed discussions with regulators involves how much description of the drug substance manufacturing process must be included in the NDA. FDA regulations require information about all the steps of the manufacturing process beginning with the "starting materials" used for the synthesis of the drug substance. Often, there is disagreement about exactly what constitutes the "starting materials." In a general sense, the "starting materials" must be well characterized commercially available substances. However, the definitions of "well characterized" and commercially available can vary and therefore it is important to come to an agreement with regulators about what constitutes acceptable starting materials for a particular drug substance as early as possible.

22391354R00143

Printed in Great Britain
by Amazon